"This workbook reads like a warm hug. Gentle and assertive at the same time, full of real and relatable examples and exercises, this book is just what we need when we struggle with one of life's biggest challenges—forgiving ourselves."

—**Janina Scarlet, PhD**, author of *Superhero Therapy*

"In this remarkable book, Dewar fearlessly explores self-blame, unraveling its toxic grip on our lives and illuminating the transformative power of self-forgiveness. With wisdom and compassion, he guides us on a journey of self-discovery, offering insights and tools to navigate regret and self-judgment. This book seamlessly blends ancient wisdom with contemporary psychology. Through relatable stories and exercises, we confront self-blame and embrace self-forgiveness. Dewar's belief in transformative potential inspires the reader to cultivate self-compassion. A must-read for anyone struggling to forgive themselves."

—**Louise McHugh**, peer-reviewed acceptance and commitment therapy (ACT) trainer, and coauthor of *A Contextual Behavioral Guide to Self*

"This book is like a warm and compassionate blanket, embracing you when you need it the most. It teaches you the possibility and power of self-forgiveness, while inviting you to embrace yourself with gentle kindness. Don't miss this transformative journey—it's a gift that both you and your inner critic deserve."

—**Rikke Kjelgaard**, psychologist, author, ACT trainer, and chief "rock'n'roller" at www.rikkekjelgaard.com

"Grant Dewar's book is a warm and playful invitation to walk the path of self-forgiveness. Grant has a unique charisma to create stories and images while describing painful processes. He offers insightful prompts so that readers can reconstruct their own narratives while exploring several aspects of self-forgiveness. I felt a beam of light on each page, and a type of catharsis throughout. I finished it filled with inspiration."

—**Stavroula Sanida, MSc**, psychologist-psychotherapist in private practice in Greece, certified trainer in functional analytic psychotherapy (FAP), and storywriter for therapeutic purposes

"*The Self-Forgiveness Workbook* is an excellent addition to anyone's toolbox! Dewar gently guides the reader through the most painful aspects of their experience. If you are overwhelmed with shame, guilt, or self-judgments, this is a workbook that can transform your relationship with yourself and your loved ones."

—**Jessica Borushok, PhD**, creator of *The ACT Therapist* YouTube channel, peer-reviewed ACT trainer, and coauthor of *The ACT Approach*

"If you get caught up in self-loathing, shame, or guilt, this book is for you. Grant's step-by-step approach will help you recognize and expand your perspective of unhelpful patterns. *The Self-Forgiveness Workbook* is filled with practical exercises and skills that will empower you to make space for painful thoughts and feelings, put energy into what truly matters, and create new ways of being with yourself and with others."

—**Sheri Turrell, PhD**, coauthor of *The Mindfulness and Acceptance Workbook for Teen Anxiety*, and creator of the Choose Your Life online course for young adults at www.lifeinbalancetherapy.ca

"One of the most challenging things we are asked to do as human beings is to forgive ourselves. It seems to be the advice we are getting everywhere. In *The Self-Forgiveness Workbook*, Grant Dewar walks us through concise, compassionate practices that make room for the pain we face with the gift of self-forgiveness. It truly is a gift you should give yourself."

—**Holly Yates, MS, LCMHC**, certified FAP trainer

"Nobody is perfect. We all have acted in blameworthy ways and have done things we dearly wish we hadn't. In this warmhearted, step-by-step workbook, Grant Dewar traces a compassionate path to self-forgiveness. In this book, you'll learn how to transform the heaviest burden into a healthy sense of self-worth. At the end of this journey, you'll feel inspired to become the worthy human that you always were, and shine!"

—**Benjamin Schoendorff**, founder of the Contextual Psychology Institute in Montreal, QC, Canada; author of several books on ACT; and international trainer

# The Self-Forgiveness Workbook

*Mindfulness and Compassion Skills to Overcome Self-Blame and Find True Self-Acceptance*

GRANT DEWAR, PHD

New Harbinger Publications, Inc.

Publisher's Note

*This publication is designed to provide accurate and authoritative information in regard to the subject matter covered. It is sold with the understanding that the publisher is not engaged in rendering psychological, financial, legal, or other professional services. If expert assistance or counseling is needed, the services of a competent professional should be sought.*

New Harbinger Publications is an employee-owned company.



New Harbinger Publications, Inc.
5720 Shattuck Avenue
Oakland, CA 94609
www.newharbinger.com



Cover design by Amy Daniel; Interior Design by Michele Waters-Kermes;

Acquired by Elizabeth Hollis Hansen; Edited by Karen Schader

---

Library of Congress Cataloging-in-Publication Data on file

Printed in the United States of America

25 24 23

10 9 8 7 6 5 4 3 2 1 First Printing

This book is dedicated to you, the traveler on the great journey that is to be taken within and then emerging back in the world refreshed, renewed, and equipped with all your unique wisdom hard won on this road of discovery.

# Contents

# Foreword

We all do things we regret. In challenging situations, we get tossed around by our thoughts and feelings, and pulled into self-defeating patterns of behavior—and we say and do things that hurt ourselves, or hurt others, or both. And when that happens, we all naturally tend to blame ourselves. We may blame ourselves for what we did do, or what we *didn't* do, or both.

The word "blame" comes to us from the ancient Latin word *blasphemare*, which means "to revile." (Of course, we also get the word "blasphemy" from this Latin root, which originally referred to reviling the name of God.) The dictionary defines "revile" as to attack abusively, prompted by anger or hatred. Isn't that basically what self-blaming entails? We launch into harsh self-judgment and self-criticism, rebuking and judging ourselves repeatedly, furious at ourselves that we could have done this or allowed that. And all too often, that self-directed anger becomes self-hatred.

But while self-blame comes naturally to all of us, it's not helpful. It doesn't help us learn from our mistakes, grow from our experiences, make amends (where that's possible), or contribute positively to the world. It keeps us stuck in a life-draining prison of our own making and often plays a big role in depression, anxiety disorders, trauma-related disorders, addictions, and many other forms of psychological suffering. Our mind hooks us and drags us back into the past—reliving all the old hurts and wounds and the bad stuff—so we get to feel it, over and over, getting more and more upset, angry, and miserable about what happened. Although this is normal, it doesn't help; all it does is suck the life out of us.

The antidote to self-blame is self-forgiveness—which *doesn't* mean saying what happened didn't matter. Self-forgiveness means giving yourself freedom from the prison of self-blame, so you can learn and grow from your mistakes, transgressions, failures, setbacks, and disappointments—and actively contribute to making the world a better place, moving forward. It's something you do not only for your own health and well-being but also to benefit your loved ones (as your prison of self-blame also impacts negatively on them).

Grant Dewar has written an excellent, practical, deeply compassionate workbook that will take you step-by-step through all the skills you need for self-forgiveness. As you work through these pages, you will learn how to take the power and impact out of harsh self-judgment, open up to make room for painful feelings, disentangle yourself from painful memories, be kind and supportive to yourself, learn from the past, get in touch with your values, and take action to build a better life for yourself and your loved ones.

You're in good hands, so appreciate the journey.

—Dr. Russ Harris

Author of *The Happiness Trap* and *When Life Hits Hard*

CHAPTER 1

# Be Present for Your Story

You have picked up this workbook to heal your relationship with yourself. Because you condemn or judge yourself harshly, you are seeking help to identify, make peace with, and possibly transform your pain. Your desire to escape from pain is understandable and universal. Painful feelings are your heart's way of crying out for relief.

Your heart's call is asking you to brave the pain of your story, which tends to lead you into a maze of pain. So naturally, entering that maze seems like a crazy thing to do. You may fear that you will encounter a monster there, but your attempts to escape from pain, distract your attention, or ignore the inner struggle leave your problem unresolved. There is a voice inside that tells you horrible things about yourself. This critical, judgmental, even cruel voice is telling you about a "monster" within. This voice is your *inner critic.* You think it speaks the truth. But consider this: what if your inner critic has produced this monster to guard your deepest pain? For so long, you have mistaken this voice for an ally and regarded the monster as an enemy. Your journey is to transform that critic into a kind, supportive voice. You can get that protective monster to work for you, not against you. Then you can reclaim your truth, your treasure—*you*—from the maze of pain.

You feel called to do this because, in the center of the maze, your authentic self resides. Pain is hiding who you are. It is also your heart appealing to you, asking for your attention. Pain is therefore a call to action. If you listen and heed the call by telling your story, you can discover self-forgiveness—and live beyond your story's pain.

In this way, self-forgiveness is alchemy, transforming what seems worthless about you into the gold of your authentic self. This change requires courage and deep honesty. As you embark on this journey, I encourage you to have faith in yourself. That faith can be transformative, as your hidden pain moves from suffering to meaning.

# The Power of Your Story

This self-forgiveness journey is the story of discovering your authentic self. This self contains all your experience, all your possibility, and all that you encompass. You are not just a star, or even a galaxy of stars, but a universe entirely of itself, so powerful beyond measure—and yet so vulnerable in this moment.

At the core of all our stories is survival in a bountiful but harsh universe, a seemingly ordered but actually random universe. As humans, we are beings who know our own thoughts, and that means we are storytellers. Human knowledge expresses itself in some form of storytelling that can be passed on. Even though many animals (including orcas, apes, chimpanzees, orangutans, and crows) can teach their offspring certain skills, tools, pathways, ways of hunting, food sources, and the difference between enemies and allies, humans are the only creatures that can reflect on this process of knowledge creation. We reflect through storytelling. We tell not only stories of fact but also stories of fiction, myth, legend, and eulogies, which can move us more powerfully than mere fact. This power lies in the deep truths of metaphor and representations of emotional connection.

Yet human knowing and storytelling is a double-edged sword. It is incredibly productive: one person can tell stories to billions of people, which can motivate them to action. But as we have experienced the age of media (printed, online, or through social media apps), we know that stories can also cause fear, division, strife, rivalry, and destruction. We have seen this side of its power exploited by business, by government, and by motivated and influential individuals.

What comes to mind when you think about the power of storytelling?

______________________________________________

______________________________________________

______________________________________________

______________________________________________

______________________________________________

Does it make you feel nervous, empowered, strong, overwhelmed? Describe several feelings you have in response to storytelling.

______________________________________________

______________________________________________

______________________________________________

______________________________________________

We shape what happens in our environment into stories to help us do a number of things. A story reduces the amount of unnecessary detail we need to remember. Without this summation, our brain circuitry would be overloaded. We need to be able to make sense of what happened; this process helps us respond and learn from those events. We need to be able to tell complex stories to others in simple, effective ways to get their assistance. In the huge amount of ongoing change in your environment, you need stories to help you:

- find the best way to respond and navigate through change;
- choose responses that work and provide outcomes you can manage;
- learn, remember, and replicate those responses when you experience those challenges again;
- find what works within the context of the challenges and circumstances you face; and
- be able to pass what you learn to those you love or care for, or who are part of your community.

Storytelling informs your awareness of what is happening to you in the environment. Stories give you the shorthand version of events, so you can make sense of how complex events fit into your worldview. Stories then help inform and formulate your responses. Let's explore your experience of stories a bit.

In one sentence, describe an event or circumstance you recently experienced.

______________________________________________________________

______________________________________________________________

Now tell the story of that event or circumstance, including how it affected you, how you responded, what the outcome was, and what you will do if it happens again.

________________________________________

________________________________________

________________________________________

________________________________________

________________________________________

Circle whether the story you told:

*caused pain* *seemed workable* *went well*

Stories can be painful, workable, or go well. A lot depends on the storytelling. Storytelling is also a double-edged sword on a personal level. On one hand, if your story reflects your circumstance accurately and is based on a useful understanding of the world and its workings, then responding in ways that will work out and benefit you becomes possible. On the other hand, if your story does not reflect your circumstances, and you have misunderstood how or why something is currently happening, then your responses will be totally different and could harm you and others. For example, when you are arguing with your spouse, you might not hear their point as it is and what it means to them. Instead, you could be responding to a fight that is years old—fighting with your spouse as if they were your parent who belittled you as a teenager. Or your anger at the person who bumped into you is not justified, because you mistook them for your school bully, when, in fact, they are preoccupied looking for a lost child and did not see you.

According to *relational frame theory*, humans make connections between seemingly random events (Barnes-Holmes et al. 2001). This ability is a powerful survival tool for learning and adaptation. Think about this example: Two people may attend a concert and after the event see a fight occur. One may see the fight as an extension of the excitement of the show (because they are a risk taker); the other may be horrified and distressed (because they want to feel safe and secure). Which person do you think will attend another concert? Most likely it will be the risk taker. The person who seeks safety and security may stop attending concerts, even though they were not involved in the fight and loved the show.

Think about a similar experience for you. Call to mind an incident that has long since passed but is still affecting your decision making and behavior in a way that might not be useful to you now.

What was the incident?

________________________________________

________________________________________

________________________________________

________________________________________

How did that experience impact or change your behavior? Perhaps you decided to confront people more often, or you isolated to avoid experiencing it again, or you decided something about the way the world works. Write down how you responded to the incident.

________________________________________

________________________________________

________________________________________

________________________________________

________________________________________

Overall, what is the lesson you learned from the incident?

________________________________________

________________________________________

________________________________________

________________________________________

How has that lesson been useful?

How has that lesson limited you?

Is this change in behavior something you have hidden from others, or even yourself until now? If so, write about why you wanted to hide it.

What reflections do you have after answering these questions?

You may have chosen a more mundane incident to describe for this exercise, or you may have chosen a painful one. But the story you chose shows how you can continue to live from a place of pain, even though the original incident that hurt you is far in the past.

Pain from your past no longer serves its initial purpose. That is why self-forgiveness depends on being willing to contact and understand the pain you are still experiencing. Once pain is contacted and understood, you can navigate your complex experience of life challenges in better ways. Through storytelling, this workbook will take into account your life circumstances as it outlines effective responses. You will have a guide to examine and assess the responses you have taken to soothe pain, responses that you may regret or condemn yourself for.

No matter how deep your self-blame, I want you to know that self-forgiveness is not only possible—it is both entirely natural and needed. It is the key to a thriving life. We need self-forgiveness because we discover our way through life by trial and error, like a baby learning to walk. A baby falls down a lot before they understand balance, weight shifts, and objects in their way. As we grow, we experiment with life and learn by our mistakes so that we can do it better next time. Healthy environments encourage us to do this. Even processes of development in the sciences and engineering show the importance of making informed errors, testing things to destruction, entering into critical debates, and reviewing others' findings, so new ways can be found, tested, and proven useful.

I hope you can see how essential it is to make mistakes. Through our mistakes, missteps, and failures, we can learn and apply the skills of how to forgive ourselves.

# The Impossible Choices in Your Story

Humans tend to believe we have the power to control life's outcomes. Yet we live in a complex universe where strange and unpredictable things happen constantly. This unpredictability can throw choices our way that may seem impossible to navigate.

Impossible choices can show up as moral dilemmas. You may have experienced, or be in the midst of, a moral dilemma in a situation presenting choices or obligations that won't lead to an outcome that aligns with what you value. You must make a decision or act in some way to respond, but the only options open to you somehow violate what is important to you. These impossible dilemmas can leave you feeling hooked into responses you don't even want to consider. Such hooks are not as simple as a battle between the "good" choice and the "evil" choice. You may have to make a choice between two goods or the lesser of two evils. Here are some examples:

- When planning a busy weekend, do you disappoint family by turning down a dinner invitation, or do you disappoint friends by saying no to concert tickets?
- Do you take a job that requires a lot of travel, or do you turn it down and keep searching for one that will allow more at-home family time?
- Do you choose to work long hours for the income, or do you work less so you can be present at your children's events?
- Do you log fewer hours for a client and not do your best work in order to keep the project on budget?
- Do you take time to care for yourself or do you spend time taking care of family?
- Say you have a business that supports a community of workers and customers, but your health is suffering. Do you accept an acquisition offer that will benefit you but close the business?
- Do you stay in a relationship that does not meet your needs? You may have tried to work on things, but your partner is settled into how things are.
- Do you stay in the family home that everyone loves but that you can barely afford to maintain?
- Do you continue to be the person who manages scarce finances while your partner spends without a plan?

Each of these decisions leads to an outcome. They may leave you burdened in ways you did not expect. The choice to repair your relationship with a spouse may lead to disconnection with friends who become offended by your priorities. The job with travel may pay important bills, but you lose connection with family events where you are missed. Your missing that school concert may be something a child remembers for the rest of their life.

You may experience personal and internal dilemmas where no one but you is hurt. You may have been offered an opportunity, but turned it down. Now you regret not taking that risk. You may have wanted to ask someone on a date, but not summoned the courage to approach them. You may have taken a safe job rather than pursued a business idea. Often there's no right or wrong answer. However, when you make a choice and take an action that ends in distress or disaster, it is possible to be hooked by that for life—unless you forgive yourself. Let's explore how you might be hooked by an impossible decision you made.

Using the examples as inspiration, describe a situation that required you to make a decision that hurt you, or others, in some way.

______________________________________________

______________________________________________

______________________________________________

______________________________________________

______________________________________________

______________________________________________

What part of that story are you paying attention to most, right now?

______________________________________________

______________________________________________

______________________________________________

In this moment, what thoughts, feelings, and physical sensations are arising?

Thoughts: *I had no idea what I was doing,* or, *How could I have been so stupid?*

______________________________________________

______________________________________________

______________________________________________

Feelings: *Anger, sadness, regret, hope, frustration*

Physical sensations: *Tension in my shoulders, butterflies in my stomach, tightness in my chest, cramps, feeling cold or hot*

Describe your sense of self in relationship to this decision. How do you regard yourself as a result?

How have you been expressing your inner feelings about this choice?

*I say really nasty things to myself in the shower when I think about it.* Or, *I kicked a chair right afterward, and every time I think about it my fists clench.* Or, *I have been complaining a lot at work about little things, but never mention what's really bothering me.*

________________________________________

________________________________________

________________________________________

________________________________________

Are you doing anything about this choice? What is your behavior?

*I am going along with the decision, but everything in me wants to run the other way.* Or, *Trying to preserve my reputation requires me to tell little lies constantly.*

________________________________________

________________________________________

________________________________________

What is motivating you? In other words, what are the values beneath the impossible dilemma?

*I value independence, but I need this job,* or, *I value integrity, but I must keep a professional appearance.* Or, *I value intimacy, but when I see my spouse I feel like I've been punched in the gut.*

________________________________________

________________________________________

________________________________________

________________________________________

What is the context for this experience?

*It arises whenever I start to relax, like in the shower.* Or, *Whenever I go near that photo gallery, our family portrait flashes before my eyes.* Or, *When I go near the café that used to be my favorite, I think of the disturbing conversation we had there.*

_______________

_______________

_______________

_______________

_______________

What relationship, family, community, and societal factors are affected by this choice?

*I can't go out dancing anymore.* Or, *I shifted from my group of friends.* Or, *I want to move to another state to get away from all these reminders.*

_______________

_______________

_______________

_______________

_______________

Your responses to burdens like the one you just explored may cause you pain. Please try to stay with it, and with this workbook. When you turn toward pain-relieving behaviors, they can become their own obstacles to healing. Obsessive thinking, unremitting self-criticism, overwhelming shame, self-medicating with either prescription or nonprescription substances, avoidance, procrastination, affairs, risk taking, and other self-harming behaviors might distance you from pain, but they also distance you from yourself. One of the most common responses to pain is to send a part of yourself into exile.

# Exiled from Your Story

We all experience deep pain from life events. A common response is to numb yourself to this experience so you can shut it out of your mind and get on with life. This response is a form of internal exile, in which you send key parts of your inner life and your identity to a remote, secret island within. You refuse to think about, for example, the dreams you had as a child or what you really want for your life. But your exiled inner self is chiseled in stone somewhere within you. When you have suppressed or rejected an important aspect of who you are, it will find a way to make its exile felt. Consider Lisette's experience.

*Lisette was a caring mother and a great coworker. She was always the giver. When coworkers needed to leave early due to family emergencies, she would take on the extra time. She was the one preparing the last-minute side dishes when more people than anticipated showed up for family gatherings.*

*Inside she felt exhausted and yet was conflicted by being exhausted. She refused to allow herself to rest because that would be selfish. The "selfish" part of her was screaming to be attended to, but Lisette refused to listen and pretended that part of her didn't exist. As a result, Lisette shut down and banished her own needs into exile.*

Like Lisette, is there a part of you screaming for attention while you refuse to listen? If so, let's explore how you might, at this moment, be an exile in your own life in some important way that might include various aspects of your life needs:

- Acknowledging your self-worth and quality of engagement with life
- Nurturing your mental health and spiritual growth
- Maintaining your physical health, nutrition, rest, and sleep
- Managing your finances
- Developing your career, work, business
- Building relationships, family and community connection

Write down your experience of a part of you that is exiled. It can help to name this part. For example, Lisette named it "Selfish." If you banished your dreams of becoming a musician, you might name it "Allegro."

Name of your banished part: ____________________

Why you named it this: ____________________

____________________

____________________

____________________

Describe how the pain of this exiled part affects you and your life. It may be pain from the original incident that made you banish this part of yourself, or the pain you experience recalling it right now. *Sometimes my shame feels so suffocating that I don't want to leave the house. That stupid part of me that made bad decisions in my youth needs to stay hidden, so I always try to avoid the things that remind me of that time in my life.*

____________________

____________________

____________________

____________________

____________________

You are experiencing pain that will not go away and only you know about. If you are experiencing resistance to this exercise, ask yourself, *Who else can help me resolve it if I do not even disclose it to myself?* I encourage you to write down any additional thoughts and feelings that arise when you think of the parts of yourself you have exiled.

____________________

____________________

____________________

____________________

____________________

This self-disclosure is the beginning of your work to resolve pain and suffering. You can step outside automatic reactions to the strong memories, sensations, and emotions. All you need is the space for a respectful process of reflection, which this workbook provides. A space that can begin to tone down harsh, judgmental self-criticism. A space for developing a more useful perspective on yourself.

## Making Room for Your Painful Story

The stories that tend to influence us the most are accounts that reflect pain and suffering. In order to respond to those stories in a way that supports you, give them respectful and objective attention. A story is not a final truth. Instead, a story may help you uncover important formative events that may have influenced your approach to life, such as your attitude about managing money. While these approaches may have been protective in some ways, they may be limiting in others. For example, the way you manage money could have a deep impact on your estimate of your self-worth and deservingness of love. A story can have many different meanings and uses depending on the perspective you take. Consider Lani's story regarding her money monster.

*Lani's family had been refugees who lost everything. They had to rebuild their lives from nothing in a new land, so as she grew up she watched her parents work long, hard, grinding hours to build a new life. They didn't have time for her, or to enjoy much of anything. As a result, Lani hated making sacrifices for financial security. She had spent her young adulthood running from money management, even as she built a comfortable life as an engineer. When she was asked to put together a project budget and present it to the finance manager, Lani was paralyzed by feelings of shame. She felt like an impostor as she put together the budget. Her inner critic told her: "If the finance manager could see who I 'really' am, she would laugh at my budget."*

By being able to observe her inner experience now, in the presence of a painful past story, Lani was able to give attention to her many inner layers. Let's follow Lani's story as you explore the inner monster you have been avoiding.

Describe a situation where you feel stuck in a way that is unexpected, and perhaps seems unreasonable for the circumstances.

*Lani earns a good salary and pays her bills on time. She can manage money, but she feels so much shame about relating with it that she doesn't want to present a work budget to anyone.*

________________________________________

________________________________________

________________________________________

________________________________________

________________________________________

________________________________________

What is your inner critic saying about the situation?

In Lani's case, it was: *Chasing money too closely will make you lose everything that's important to you.*

________________________________________

________________________________________

________________________________________

________________________________________

Now make some space for this critic to tell its side of the story. Know that its view is only part of your experience and does not truly define you. What story is your inner critic telling?

*Lani could see herself as a little girl, left with neighbors while her parents worked long hours. She had needed love, but felt alone in the world because her parents never again wanted to be without financial assets and means. But while they worked all hours for financial security, she lost their presence in her life.*

What emotions, thoughts, images, or sensations do you perceive in your inner critic's story?

*Lani realized that she feared anyone hearing her budget presentation would see her as a lost, lonely little girl.*

Is there a different way you might respond to this story? Rather than avoiding or exiling a part of you that is in pain, what else might you do?

*Lani knew she had to give that pained little girl within herself the love that had been missing from her parents.*

With the courage to embrace this process, your inner critic may show you what the monster within is really trying to protect. Lani's objective attention to her painful story allowed her to respectfully discover an unmet core need. By looking with two perspectives (as a professional and as a pained eight-year-old), she gained understanding and wisdom. She could see how managing money well did not automatically mean she would lose connection and love. Similarly, you can consider your stories respectfully, and also realize they are not written in stone.

The hard truth is that, as a living being, you need pain. Pain is an indicator of stress, disease, danger. Pain shows something that you need to pay attention to and respond to. If all experience of pain were removed from you today, it would be a disaster, physically and emotionally. The loss of a sense of pain might leave you with a body broken beyond repair within a matter of a few weeks, and possibly dead long before your time. You wouldn't get the signal that something needs attention—especially medical attention. This is as true for our mental health and psychological care.

A path of no pain would leave you numb to the feedback you need to correct your course. Internally, you would be in an emotional limbo, unable to detect important compass signals that can help point you in the right direction. Ultimately, without pain, you can't defend what you love. It may become lost to you, with no way to rediscover it. Pain is important to the process of discovering what you deeply value. Through it, you can discover the values that will become enduring guides for your unique life journey (Barnes-Holmes, Hayes, and Dymond 2001).

## Your Relationship to Memories of Pain

Your first response to pain might be to flinch, avoid hurt, and fight back to protect your wounds. This response continues to happen when pain is remembered, perceived, or witnessed. Our memories of pain are part of the healing process. They are present in the stories you tell yourself and in the stories you share. They are even found in the great stories of our culture, whether they be spiritual teachings, adventure, drama, comedy, or myths and legends.

Even when you're not currently in danger, you can react to what you think and remember as if you were in a life-threatening situation. Most often, you will respond to this pain with overwhelming emotions. Anger, distress, humiliation, numbness, astonishment, and so on may arise without control. Be reassured: even though these initial reactions may sometimes seem out of control, they are normal.

The challenge is therefore not to eliminate painful memories from your life. Instead, I encourage you to correctly identify what pain is telling you. To meet this challenge, pain needs to be openly examined. Your pain exists for a purpose. Your ability to detect painful events will allow for healthy avoidance of traps and pitfalls. In this way, you will build new ways to approach life. To learn new skills. To build friendships. To end unhealthy relationships. To take on the challenges right for you.

Please do not automatically judge the experience of pain. Perhaps you tell yourself there's something wrong with you for feeling it. Judgment leads immediately to self-criticism that is harsh and sometime paralyzing. This judgmental criticism is a muddied response, which in turn makes it hard for you to understand pain, and harder to work with it and become flexible in its presence. That is how you can get stuck in long-term, self-reinforcing cycles of distress.

You can learn to respond to pain in a way that works. The first step is to develop a clear understanding of your pain and its origins. Only then can you start to discover what is causing your ongoing experience of pain. You can find this clarity through the process of self-forgiveness as a response to emotional pain. Forgiving yourself is about loving yourself. You can express this love as you hold your pain with authentic openness, interest, acceptance, and an intention to bring a compassionate light to the darkness you have experienced.

## Writing Your Way to Self-Forgiveness

As you work on your own experiences of pain, know that the people I help—those who do this work—benefit from being able to reflect on their experience through writing. As they explicitly describe the hurt they've experienced in the past, as well as acknowledging the criticisms and judgments they experience now, they gain the ability to reflect and gather important insights into who they are and what they want in life. While their stories can help you get started, there is no need to compare your experiences with others' experiences. Your experience is unique and worthy of understanding in its own right. With understanding, you can decide what actions are needed for you. The discovery of pain requires courage, but the promise of discovering you—who you really are—makes this process worthwhile. Everyone needs forgiveness in their lives, and we all have courageous work to do, in a way that reflects our personal values. Here is how Madelyn navigated the process of looking at her pain.

*Madelyn was finding the details of arranging her children's visitation time with her ex-husband increasingly overwhelming. Her younger daughter was blissfully unaware of any problem, yet her older daughter was difficult whenever she was to spend time at her dad's, creating problems that forced Madelyn and her ex-husband to interact. It was obvious that her older girl wanted Madelyn to reconcile and for her mom and dad to be together again. Madelyn felt so guilty about the family being split.*

*She took time to reflect on this experience and wrote about what was happening. As she read it back to herself, she felt a tightness in her chest and felt the weight of all the stress that had led to the separation: lack of respect, feeling controlled, inability to express her emotions in the marriage, and financial burdens she had to shoulder. Madelyn acknowledged that all this was part of the story of her pain.*

*As she paid attention to her body using a meditative practice, she found tightness in her brow, a knot in her chest, and pain in her abdomen. Each was part of the distress she had experienced in her relationship. She could see images of the arguments that had led to their separation, and then she could see images of her eldest daughter's distress.*

By holding both of these stories, Madelyn discovered just how sharp the experience of inner conflict was. She was so busy trying to get through the practicalities of handing her children over to her ex-husband that she had exiled her sense of confusion, sadness, and sharp anger. As she made space for these feelings and became present in this experience, she saw what was most important. Madelyn realized that she needed to form a more respectful response to her own pain, as well as her older daughter's and her ex-husband's.

Now it's your turn. As you do this exercise, keep your inner exile in mind. Identify a life event where the pain of this inner exile has affected you in a way that is limiting or ineffective. Describe the scenario.

______________________________________________

______________________________________________

______________________________________________

______________________________________________

______________________________________________

______________________________________________

______________________________________________

Now reread the scenario you have just written down, perhaps speaking it out loud to yourself. Consider and write down what thoughts, emotions, and sensations you experience in your body as you speak this experience.

Thoughts (for example, *I too am in pain; If I observe the exchange, I see a woman trying to do her best in difficult circumstances*):

________________________________________

________________________________________

________________________________________

Emotions (for example, sadness, anger, distress, frustration, fear):

________________________________________

________________________________________

________________________________________

Bodily reactions (for example, tight chest, fluttering heart, headache, tension across shoulders, sweating):

________________________________________

________________________________________

________________________________________

Now take a deep breath.

Allow yourself to be safe in this present moment.

Breathing steadily and comfortably.

Allow all your experience to be as it is—allow it space.

Breathe into feeling that space until you notice that you can contain all this experience.

How was it to be present with your thoughts, emotions, and bodily sensations? Write about your experience.

______________________________________________________________________

______________________________________________________________________

______________________________________________________________________

______________________________________________________________________

______________________________________________________________________

An important part of this process is being present with yourself through self-compassion. At its simplest, self-compassion is considering your suffering and pain with love, respect, and acceptance. Begin exploring this space, as it is a foundation for healing. As you continue to explore through the course of this workbook, you will discover the courage and openheartedness to be a true observer to your inner experience. You will be given skills to suspend harsh, critical judgment and make space for compassionate self-acceptance. Your stories and scenarios are offering opportunities for self-compassion as a way of healing through self-forgiveness. Let's keep going.

## Navigating the Wonders and Fears

As you begin to navigate the experience of pain, know this: you are not broken. This is in spite of your story and all that your mind, your context, and your experience might say. Why? The answer is: because your being alive and reading this book at this moment is a miracle, whether or not you are a person of science, faith, or spirituality.

It is worth contemplating. The odds of life existing in this universe are impossibly small. Within that small space, the odds that you exist are billions, perhaps trillions, to one. Yet here you are, reading this book. If anything else existed by such a chance, you would behold it as a miracle beyond worth. So please consider how special it is that you exist and what an opportunity that is. And in that context, you can hold your pain with a respectful and compassionate perspective.

Consider what it would take to construct a replica of you, a duplicate that was absolutely the same as you. What would that cost? Is it even possible? Write down your thoughts.

_______________

_______________

_______________

With this perspective, consider your real worth. While your inner critic might say you are worthless, is this true, given the rare opportunity you have to be alive? Write down your responses.

_______________

_______________

_______________

For a moment, contemplate the priceless wonder that is you and the gift of your life. Write down three things that are wondrous about you.

1. _______________
2. _______________
3. _______________

Even with this experience of being a living miracle, as a human your mind is oriented toward fending off disaster. As a species, our history of survival keeps us oriented to being aware of, and responding to, endless catastrophe. The result is that your mind will search out what may be disastrous without, as well as within. Pain is a reminder of possible disaster looming, especially mortality.

Avoiding your pain or distracting yourself from feeling it may do as much, or more, damage than the originating cause. Why is this so? Why does this seem to be a feature of the human condition? That which keeps you alive may do so for this moment. For example, you might be doing a really important job and get it right 98 percent of the time. But if you get it wrong 2 percent of the time, those errors might cause you to lose that job. All the things you did right may not save your job. The same can be true for life. All the good things you experience keep you alive for this moment. However, your life can cease at any time—a permanent and irreversible outcome. This inherent risk means your adverse experiences grip your attention far more than your good experiences. But dwelling on the negative can skew your attention until your responses to pain are unhelpful and unworkable. This is especially the case for unnecessary avoidance or distraction. Here's how this came up for Charlize.

*Charlize was extremely fearful of the addiction in her family. She had horrible recollections of the physical distress after her mother's intoxication caused a car accident. Then there was the time her brother got into a violent fight outside a nightclub. She blamed herself deeply for failing to help them stop drinking and using substances. Although she experienced chronic pain due to an old sports injury, she avoided any pain medication, fearing that she might slip into addiction and never recover. Despite this distress, she decided to wait for corrective surgery in six months. Yet every day, her pain stopped her from being active, and sometimes she couldn't get out of bed. Her automatic thought was* Am I an addict too because I need pain relief? *The warring sensations of pain and fear of addiction were driving Charlize to despair.*

When you believe you have failed, were mistaken, or have in some way caused harm, this innate instinct to avoid or distract may grip you, leaving you unable to forgive yourself. This instinct told Charlize: "You cannot risk taking pain medication, or you will end up like your mother and brother—addicted beyond help." The distress arising from a fear like this, of repeating your own mistakes or those of others, may become a focus of your attention, resulting in a harsh inner critic that belittles or harshly reminds you of your mistakes and failings. Charlize's inner critic constantly told her: "Don't be so weak, be stronger than the pain," even as the pain began taking over her life. She began working through the process in this workbook, and here's how her experience of this inner conflict unfolded.

*Charlize used a mindful breathing exercise to scan her body and her inner experience. This exercise helped her make room for her physical pain, so that slowly she could also make room for her thinking and feeling experiences. She then focused on the knotted confusion in her thinking about addiction. By breathing into it and making room for the confusion, Charlize noticed just how distressed she felt about her mother and brother, and all the pain she experienced as a result of their addictions. She realized that their pain was not hers, and she withdrew from feeling their pain. Instead, she focused on her own fears and needs. Her physical pain was valid; it was not manufactured. She was not seeking opiates for fun. Her pain would most likely be relieved by a skillful operation, so she decided to take opiates leading up to the surgery and for postoperative recovery—according to the prescription and dose. It would be okay.*

Now it's your turn to explore. Find a safe place where you can meditate without being disturbed either by external factors or by your own discomfort. Find a comfortable posture that suits your physical needs.

Now notice any particular tensions or responses in your body. Write them down.

____________________________________________________________

____________________________________________________________

____________________________________________________________

What do you fear about yourself or others or circumstances around you? Name the most pressing fears.

____________________________________________________________

____________________________________________________________

____________________________________________________________

____________________________________________________________

What behaviors do you engage in to avoid or distract from that pressing fear? Do you work overtime? Scroll on your phone? Drink? Sleep all day?

____________________________________________________________

____________________________________________________________

____________________________________________________________

____________________________________________________________

Breathe into this awareness, allowing the space to open up around this fear and these behaviors, making room for them. What does it feel like within this space?

Expand this space to allow the fear to be as it is. Nothing about it needs to change. You can stay aware of this fear and your responses to it. Allow your consciousness to expand to whatever size it wants to hold all of your experiences. What does it feel like to be aware of you, as you are?

Now consider what the origin of your fear is. Perhaps the cause of your fear arises as a memory, a story, or a feeling. Let this origin story unfold within the space of your awareness. Then write it down.

Knowing this origin story, ask yourself whether there is another way of responding to this experience. Perhaps you can hold it rather than avoid or distract from it. Write down other, more helpful ways you can take care of you.

______________________________________________

______________________________________________

______________________________________________

______________________________________________

______________________________________________

You have been trying to take care of your pain by exiling it. But you are now learning new ways of caring for you. As you close this meditation, take a deep breath and remember that it is a wonder to be alive. The story of your fear is not all there is to your life. You can grow beyond your pain, and forgive yourself, by holding space for who you are—all of you—including your important relationships with other people.

## Taking on Other People's Voices

Your story of the origin of your fear likely involves other people. As social creatures, we have a default setting: We have developed over millennia in social settings. We are meant to be together. To live in a community. More than any other species on this planet, we rely on the goodwill of parents, family, and community to stay alive. Therefore, we respond automatically to social cues.

As infants, our senses awaken through attachment and bonding with other people. At an early age, our first thoughts are to confirm relationships. We know that we are reliant on others for our well-being, and we are therefore very aware of the need to fit in and comply. As we grow up, we are therefore constantly self-regulating and self-examining to ensure that we follow the rules that will enable us to survive in our social settings.

An unfortunate consequence of this self-examination is that as children we may learn to blame ourselves for things we cannot control. Why do we do this? Self-blame can provide us with at least a tiny experience of control. This sense of control is strangely comforting in a sometimes capricious and chaotic universe. So children might blame themselves for the breakup of their parents, the death of a loved one, or the loss of a pet. These experiences can have a marked effect on your life. Blaming yourself for events like these, or for someone else's harmful behavior, is not helpful beyond giving you a sense of control. It leads to a harshly self-critical internal voice. Here's how Leah experienced this.

> *Leah was really distressed that her divorce was being finalized. Her culture frowned deeply on divorce; women from her homeland would never think of leaving their husbands—no matter what. Even though she had been educated in the West, lived there for decades, and now taught in higher education, the voice of her grandmother rang in her inner consciousness:* "You are shaming your family." *As a result, Leah blamed herself for her marriage's failure, even though her husband had been neglectful and self-absorbed all along.*

Do you have a critical voice ringing in your mind that sounds like someone important to you? What personality does that inner voice have? It could be a parent, uncle or aunt, sibling, or grandparent. It could be a critical schoolteacher, the leader of a clique that excluded you, a bully, an ex-lover or partner. Write down their name and the role they played in your past, or even play presently.

________________________________________

________________________________________

________________________________________

________________________________________

What is this voice from the past saying now, in your thoughts? It might sound like this: "*You are a reject, you are a failure, you will never get what you want in life, you procrastinate all the time.*"

________________________________________

________________________________________

________________________________________

As you will discover throughout this workbook, often there is a grain of truth covered by the pain you experience. Think of your pain like mud concealing an oyster. You just need to dig a bit and open the oyster to find the pearl you seek. This pearl is a lesson you need for your life pathway.

*Leah had always respected her grandmother. Not all their interactions involved criticism, and even when it came, it was clear her grandmother was trying to give life guidance based on her experience in the culture she knew. So Leah imagined what the heart of her grandmother's concern might be and asked herself how that concern might be expressed in more respectful terms. She realized that her grandmother was emphasizing how important family is. And Leah agreed, family was important to her also. But a family that constantly fights and is distressed is not a good one to raise children in. In this way, Leah could see that her divorce was a way to take care of her family. She was acting in a way that supported her values after all.*

Now it is your turn. Reimagine someone's harsh criticism as if it were a respectfully made and valid observation, such as: *You want to be accepted by people you respect. You want to make your project work. You want to build a financial foundation for a future goal. Completing a task will liberate you to do something new.* Write down what is at the heart of what they are saying.

______________________________________________________________________

______________________________________________________________________

______________________________________________________________________

______________________________________________________________________

______________________________________________________________________

______________________________________________________________________

Consider how that respectful approach might change your response to that voice. Do you feel any physical changes in your body? Are alternate or surprising emotions arising? What new thoughts are coming to mind? Do you see new images of an alternate experience? Describe anything that occurs to you.

_______________________________________________

_______________________________________________

_______________________________________________

_______________________________________________

_______________________________________________

_______________________________________________

_______________________________________________

This exercise can be challenging, but now you have a new, respectful response to your inner voice. This important skill will help you broaden and deepen your range of experiences. Before, your response was likely too burdensome. A respectful interpretation of inner criticism can help you quiet that monster, understand what it has been guarding, and ultimately use that treasure to build your new approach to life.

# Feeling Stuck in Pain

Earlier in this chapter, I asked you to consider that pain has a purpose. It is sharing a message that may transform your life. So far, we have begun the process of facing painful stories. But going through the pain to reach that place of transformation can be really difficult. You may have done something that hurts you so profoundly that you experience deep injury to your moral sense of self. You may have transgressed against social values, personal values, or family values. You may be asking *Why should I be forgiven? What I did is unforgivable.*

Consider what might happen if you take what you believe to be unforgivable and put it on trial. Although most of the actions people blame themselves for are not real crimes, they treat themselves worse than criminals, placing themselves in a jail of inner shame for years, if not a lifetime. Yet they have never given themselves a fair trial. If it had been a real offense, what would the fine be? How much time would you really serve? If you did pay the fine, do you need to pay that over and over again? If you serve your time, would you serve that over and over again too?

Write about how long you have served this prison term you have sentenced yourself to. How long do you plan to punish yourself? How long should it have lasted? Would you punish a good friend that long?

______________________________________________________________________

______________________________________________________________________

______________________________________________________________________

______________________________________________________________________

______________________________________________________________________

______________________________________________________________________

Having contemplated your self-imposed prison, is it time you stepped into freedom? Sometimes we do need to make restoration, recompense, or restitution, to genuinely apologize to others—and sometimes to no one else but ourselves.

*Madelyn had to balance her commitment to family with her commitment to her safety and the safety of her children. She had paid the price well and truly by trying all she could to make the relationship work. But it couldn't work. That was her fine. Her next step was to walk into her freedom.*

Like Madelyn, if you are living to meet the standards of others, without the balance of living according to your own values, you will feel a lot of pain in the form of anxiety, depression, self-doubt. Culture, family, and relationship are strong drivers of behaviors that may cause deep moral injury. For example, say your family strongly expected you to marry, build wealth, and have children raised within the family's religious tradition and cultural values, but you felt more inspired to devote your career to solving a major societal problem than you did to living out their formula. You may suppress or not listen to subtle warning signs arising from your own values that conflict with their expectations. Instead, the social pressures from your family may triumph over what you want for your life, causing you to enter a marriage and stay in that relationship to keep them happy, despite a spouse who does not want you to work outside the home or who opposes your dream of leading a nonprofit. This is how deep moral injury is experienced.

Stuck pain is often the result of moral injury: a conflict between your values and someone else's values. It has the quality of a deep warning, a continuing alarm. The longer you ignore it, the more you avoid it, the more it will keep you stuck.

*Derrick was from a family that really wanted to see him happy in a relationship and having children. He met a woman who seemed to check all his family's boxes, but he didn't feel quite right about it. There was something about the way she treated others: making silly demands of restaurant servers, turning up late, and expecting things to be done for her. Just a certain arrogance.*

*They were generally happy. They seemed to have a future. After four years, however, the harsh way she treated others started to happen more and more. She was more demanding, but there were always excuses. Derrick buried his doubts deeper, along with his pain. Her needs were always first, bills started not being paid, her long hours "with friends" didn't seem to ring true. Arguments about lost time and finances consumed them. After eight years everything felt overwhelming, and he left.*

*When he finally started the process of dealing with what he had been exposed to, the realization came. That feeling at the beginning that something wasn't quite right was absolutely on target. Now after eight wasted years, the best part of himself feeling crushed, no family, no children. Disaster. He couldn't forgive himself for wasting so much time on a relationship that wasn't right from the beginning. He had ignored his own judgment to please his family. If only he had listened to the feeling when something didn't seem quite right. He felt like a fool, with such shame and so much pain.*

If Derrick allows his response to pain to be where he remains stuck, his life will not work. Grief is a useful and normal human response to a huge setback. But if he gets stuck in that grief, it becomes an *unworkable response*—because there is no way forward. He will remain in a swamp of pain. On the other hand, *workable responses* to pain help you respond to, and view, the world and yourself in a new, different, improved fashion. You can take stock of regret and shame. You can develop new values about things you previously took for granted. A rotten tooth grabs your attention when you aren't taking care of your mouth. Stub your toe on a chair, and you soon remember how valuable toes are to walking. Someone who takes advantage of you reminds you to be wise in your choice of company. These painful experiences can become reminders to take care of yourself.

When you have survived painful experiences, you can find strengths you did not previously know you had. You may discover your capabilities under adversity. Pain may give you the ability to test your ethics, morals, and capacity to improve yourself. Pain may provide you with the experience you need to develop compassion, understanding, and respect for the viewpoints of others. The experiences of pain may help you develop empathy, and both forgive and seek forgiveness. The learning gained from pain helps you understand the history of your circumstances and points you toward a preferred, valued future. In his 2016 TEDx talk, "How Love Turns Pain into Purpose," psychologist Steven C. Hayes highlights how pain and purpose are joined at the pivot point of hurt and care: "We hurt where we care, and we care where we hurt." You are on a journey through various levels of hurt, and your focus can now be on what you care about.

You have survived painful experiences. So far, we have looked at unworkable responses, including exiling yourself, avoiding and distracting yourself out of fear of pain, internalizing other people's voices, and getting stuck. So now let's start exploring workable responses. Let's explore how you are already learning from pain.

What three lessons lie within your experience of survival?

1. ________________________________________

________________________________________

2. ________________________________________

________________________________________

3. ________________________________________

________________________________________

How can these lessons help you live your life the way you want?

_______________

_______________

_______________

_______________

_______________

How do they hold you back?

_______________

_______________

_______________

_______________

_______________

As you learn to forgive yourself, allow your pain to have a compassionate space in which to heal. Your experience is normal. While your current experience of pain might not be helpful at the moment, there is a way through. Your harsh inner critic may be crippling you right now. However, when you approach it with a spacious, open, compassionate view, you can transform that crippling experience into strength.

You are a miracle that is as wondrous as life itself. You also possess a deep wisdom that will grow and be revealed as you follow your path. Respecting and loving parts of yourself that you may have held to be monsters, unlovable parts of you, or unpleasant critics, is something you can learn (Harris 2006). It is a skill you will build through the course of this workbook, and then apply throughout your life. Self-forgiveness is a catalyst that can transform many different experiences into things you can value, and guides you on your life journey. As a catalyst, self-forgiveness can be a useful skill to apply in this miracle that is the journey of your life.

CHAPTER 2

# Try on a Compassionate Lens

You may have thought and viewed something in a particular way for a long time. It has been familiar, a given, a truth. Then one day, you receive some new information, something you never knew before. Suddenly, it is as if the world has turned on its axis. Sometimes that is liberating, sometimes very disturbing. This is the power of a new perspective.

As we continue this journey, perspective-taking skills will equip you with points of view that are helpful, allowing you to be the person you want to be. A compassionate approach accepts your suffering, acknowledges that you have been carrying pain, embraces you as you are, and allows you to make the decisions you need to make (Kolts 2016). It is a lens that will help open pathways to your preferred life. *Compassionate perspective-taking* is how you can change your world with intention. In the first chapter, you have already been practicing it.

Write down one way the content in chapter 1 helped you take a compassionate perspective toward yourself.

______________________________________________

______________________________________________

______________________________________________

______________________________________________

______________________________________________

______________________________________________

Skills such as creating a quiet space for reflection, writing out difficult stories, using meditative exercises to ground you in your body, and looking for the lessons in the painful experiences are all ways to put on a compassionate lens. As a result, you can gain new information that may change the way you see the world.

Some of the most difficult experiences to engage in happen when we believe we are deeply at fault for our own pain and suffering. When you have this belief, there is a reason, and this reason needs a compassionate lens. Inclusive of what you did, what you were going through at the time, and how you felt about it, know that your actions had a reason and a context. What you did may not have turned out the way you thought it would. However, the person you were then was doing the best you could with what you had at that point in time.

The self-forgiveness process can give tools to the wise person you are now, for responding compassionately to the person you were then. Here is how Skylar navigated this.

> *Skylar was too busy in her educational counseling role. Raising two teenage boys was also really taxing. Supporting their sports teams took up time, which she did not begrudge. A fellow soccer mom befriended Skylar and started talking about the busyness of life. Soon the discussion focused solely on the needs of the new friend. Each soccer practice became an unpaid session of free relationship counseling. Skylar did not know how to free herself from this trap.*
>
> *One night, in sheer frustration, Skylar poured out her frustrations in a text to her sister—but she accidentally sent it to her fellow soccer mom, who immediately responded with seething anger. Skylar was paralyzed with shame. Although she apologized profusely, the text message had an unintended effect. At soccer practice, the other moms now cast icy stares her way. This anger continued until the end of the season. Skylar was mortified, and it was dragging her down. She was determined to forgive herself, so in a session of meditative practice, Skylar treated her wrongly texting self as she would a good friend.*
>
> *She listened to and identified the many ways she viciously criticized herself with things like* How could I be so rude? *and* How can I treat people like that?
>
> *She gave her texting self space to express her pain, frustration, and sheer exhaustion.*
>
> *She visualized giving herself a hug and sharing tears of emotional pain with her texting self.*
>
> *In that space, Skylar realized that she had not set out to hurt the fellow soccer mom. She also realized that she had not done the right thing for herself, as she had failed to set boundaries to protect herself and her time. She noticed how her inner critic began to soften and shift its emphasis.*
>
> *With perspective, Skylar felt her burden shift. She understood she was doing the best she could, but there were many things pressing upon her. Yes, amends were due for the misdirected text. However, an inner conversation was needed about professional and social boundaries with people in her life. It was time to ask: what needs to change?*

Describe a time when you tried to make something go well and it turned out badly.

How did you immediately talk to yourself about that mistake? Consider whether this was the voice of your inner critic.

Now write down how you would talk to a friend in pain and distress because of a mistake. Are you willing to do this for yourself?

How does your inner voice change when you change perspective from the you who criticizes yourself to the you who made a mistake and needs a friend?

Your ability to hold multiple perspectives at once might feel like having different voices and personalities within you. In most contexts, you will act as you typically do. But in some circumstances, you might act in ways that differ from your norm. For example, say you work in isolation doing a difficult job. On a Friday night after a hard work week, some good friends arrange a night on the town. Everyone wants to let go, and they get a bit wild. What you do that night, and the decisions you make, could be very different from your usually reserved self. Similarly, if you experienced a great loss or pain, certain circumstances may cause unusual emotions and sensations to arise. You may not feel in control of them, and therefore may act in a way that is not normal for you.

If this has happened to you, consider allowing wider context that can include your new inner experience, unfamiliar behaviors, and unexpected responses. The new skills you learn in this chapter will allow you to be more compassionate toward yourself, be more open to your experience, take an interest in what's happening within you, and become curious about these feelings, thoughts, and behaviors that are outside your norm.

## Being a Friend to Yourself

When you notice your experience and bring respect and compassion to it, you do not silence your inner critic. Compassion means to "suffer with" or "to be with suffering." Your inner critic is a part of yourself that is suffering. It is asking you to become a friend to yourself, the self experiencing pain. Think of how Skylar treated her "texting self," offering accepting and nonjudgmental companionship. She developed an inner dialogue that allowed room for her suffering. This space fostered respect, dignity, and openness, which led to insights into how she could improve her situation.

Another way to transform suffering, and become a friend to yourself, is with *mindful reflection*. Mindful reflection allows thoughts, images, emotions, and physical sensations to become things that can be observed. They can be something you are experiencing, something you have, something that is not "you" and does not define who you are. With the following practices, you can easily cultivate this ability to observe your experience.

**Mindful Attention Practice:** All you need to do is focus your attention on your breathing for five minutes. As you focus attention on your breath, you will soon find a continuous stream of thoughts, images, emotions, and physical sensations continually trying to grab your attention. Each time that happens, choose to bring your attention back to your breathing. Doing this daily, for just five minutes, has been shown to have enormous benefits. You will cultivate *mindful attention*.

Go ahead, take five minutes to try the mindful attention practice. Then write about your experience.

______________________________________________________________________

______________________________________________________________________

______________________________________________________________________

______________________________________________________________________

______________________________________________________________________

______________________________________________________________________

**Mindful Reflection Practice:** Mindful reflection takes mindful attention one step further. Focus on one aspect of your life. Each time your attention is dragged away, simply bring it back to that one aspect. You are training your attention to return to what you are reflecting on.

Throughout this workbook, I invite you to practice mindful reflection. For all the steps you take toward healing, there will be missteps, diversions, trips, and falls. You can always return your attention to healing. As we go, mindful reflection will help you consider how you got to be where you are, at any given moment. Whether you are in a moment of self-affirmation or of deep internal criticism, mindful reflection supports your ability to take a perspective that is open, interested, and curious about your journey. It is a key skill you will need to create your preferred future. Even if things are going well, it is wise to reflect on your journey and gather lessons. When things go wrong, a harsh, vile, even destructive inner critic will only harm you. To find a beneficial path forward, you will need a respectful inner dialogue, based on mindful reflection, that can uncover useful perspectives to guide your response.

With these perspectives, you will turn pain into purpose. It is a journey of developing wisdom about your response to pain. Once you cease ignoring and avoiding your pain, you gain the opportunity to hear, consider, and apply the wise messages it contains.

Here is how it works: A compassionate response is a journey of discovery as it transforms a painful experience into a source of wisdom. Mindful reflection gives you the opportunity to examine your pain as an experience you have—you can observe the pain, as it does not define you. This observation allows you to start extracting the information the pain contains. Skylar did this by being a friend to her "texting self," giving herself room to examine her painful experience of shame, and realized that she was not taking care of herself. She needed to set boundaries with people and give herself enough rest to recover energy and positivity.

Let's begin to transform pain into wisdom by putting all your experience in a place of safety and reflection. This is a space to learn what you truly value. To understand what you really want to guide your life by. As you continue to engage the practices in this workbook, you will learn to drop harsh, critical judgments about yourself and open up to your experience with compassion. As harsh inner criticism quiets, this process opens up respectful inner dialogue.

Earlier in this chapter, you considered a time when you tried to make something go well and it turned out badly. Return to your scenario, this time with a compassionate frame of mind. Treat yourself as you would a good friend. Describe what happened again. Is there another way to interpret what you went through and your response?

_______________________________________________

_______________________________________________

_______________________________________________

_______________________________________________

_______________________________________________

Does this perspective tell you anything about your valid needs? If so, write down the needs revealed by the story.

_______________________________________________

_______________________________________________

_______________________________________________

Can you identify qualities that you value about yourself from this version of the story? Write them down.

______________________________________________________________________

______________________________________________________________________

______________________________________________________________________

As you work your way through this chapter, you will refer to these questions. The process of self-forgiveness may seem awkward at first, but you will soon be proficient at it. It can help the richness of the life that lies before you unfold.

## Exploring Responses to Pain

With a compassionate lens and mindful reflection, you are courageously exploring the experience of pain in your life. Let's look at common responses to pain. They are responsible for creating your harsh, and sometimes crippling, inner critic. They become highly toxic if you take a harshly judgmental stance toward yourself. To reduce and reverse this toxicity, you will learn new ways to consider these responses to pain:

- Remorse
- Regret
- Self-blame
- Guilt
- Shame
- Self-hatred
- Self-rejection
- Self-disgust
- Self-loathing

During setbacks in life, you might notice that your inner critic's voice is amplified. Its responses have some degree of validity. However, whether those responses are healthy or not depends on the life context and consequences of those responses. Ask yourself: *Do my responses actually fit the problem?* and *Do my responses help resolve the situation?*

Your life experience is healthy if it invites learning and growth. However, if you get stuck in cycles of behavior that do not work, those behaviors can spiral into toxicity. The following discussions will help you learn how to tell the difference between what is healing and repairing, as opposed to what will cause more avoidance and toxic stagnation.

## *Remorse*

Feelings of remorse are ultimately prompts to change something. If you have acted or failed to act, and as a result caused some sort of harm or loss that might have been avoided, you may respond remorsefully. The painful outcome may be overwhelmingly distressing and weigh heavily on your conscience. This remorse may mean that you acted against the values you hold. As a result, your internal critic tends to repeat its commentary over and over.

**Excessive remorse:** Remorse that becomes toxic is characterized by a fixation on events with thoughts like *I am in constant anguish, I could have prevented that, or acted differently, or produced a better outcome*. Remorse that is excessive tends to influence the way you view your life as a whole, rather than just a specific instance. Because your thinking keeps on turning the same events and accusations over and over again, excessive remorse often leads to cripplingly low moods or excessive anxiety. You may feel drained. You are restricted in a state of obsessive inner focus. You may feel you can never do enough to compensate for your mistakes.

**Healthy remorse:** Genuine remorse sets the stage for a healthy response that works to restore both the transgression and its results. You have the opportunity to develop a deeper understanding of the causes of your distress. You can develop a deeper understanding of the hurt and damage done, and consider useful responses like accepting responsibility for actions or omissions that were its causes. You can clearly explain what happened without making excuses. You more clearly understand the suffering of whoever is the victim, including yourself. Regret may be humbling. Mindful reflection can guide your commitment to change in ways that are credible, including restoration, restitution, or compensation for the damage done. Healthy remorse ensures that such behaviors will not reoccur.

*After Derrick left his toxic relationship, he had a deep, churning sense that he had failed to be true to his values. This remorseful thinking led him to some very dark places. He ruminated over his loss of innocence and how his youthful spirit had been crushed by a relationship that didn't work. Then he started to practice self-compassion and mindfulness. When he took time to journal this experience, he realized the importance of this sense of remorse: he must never repeat that experience by entering a relationship driven by his family's expectations. He resolved to clarify what he wanted in life before he started dating again.*

Consider your remorse and circle one option:

*My remorse is excessive.* *My remorse is healthy.*

If it is excessive, write down the story behind it. As you do, consider breaking down the story into three or four key points that you can work on one at a time.

_______________

_______________

_______________

_______________

_______________

If it is healthy, what steps are you ready to take to address the remorse's cause?

_______________

_______________

_______________

Having done this, what are your mindful reflections on remorse? What have you learned about yourself by acknowledging this response?

______________________________________________

______________________________________________

______________________________________________

______________________________________________

## *Regret*

Regret differs from remorse. Regret can focus on a particular action, an inaction, an incident, or something that failed to happen. The focus includes all forms of behavior and circumstances that do not work out how you want, or how you expected. It may include your inability to take action, or lack of capacity to see opportunity, or having missed an opportunity. In the short run, you may feel the greatest regret for actions that cause someone, including you, distress. In the long run, a failure to take action tends to cause more intense distress. Regret is intensified when there is a perception that an opportunity existed to take some form of preventive or corrective action. It is also strengthened when there are clear comparisons for what would have happened differently if you had seized that opportunity. Regretful thoughts may focus on the action itself at a point in time. However, regret also may focus on what could have been, on what should be now, or on a lost alternate future. These form simple or extremely complex narratives that seem to create a parallel universe in your mind.

**Excessive regret:** Imagination coupled with a harsh inner critic may inflame your experience with never-ending scenarios. Consuming thoughts start with "What if?" and "If only," and you examine lost alternatives over and over again. This mental replay by your inner critic is a magnifying lens on the hurt and disappointment you feel. More far-reaching torture includes imagining scenarios of what could have been right now, or even what your future could have looked like. You become unable to concentrate on what you face here and now, in the present moment. Excessive regret may lead to experiences of despair, hopelessness, or paralysis.

**Healthy regret:** Each regret is an opportunity to learn, a possibility for determined action and restoration. Regret is a key platform for humanity's capacity to adapt to disaster. When you engage creatively with regret, it opens up the possibility of multiple courses of action. Regret allows you to take stock and identify new ways of responding to life circumstances. Then you can build new responses to similar events. Regret therefore provides a signpost, such as: *Stop! Don't do that again.* Or *Beware! This course of action will cause a problem.* You can create your own proverbs providing cautionary tales that arise from regrets.

*Lisette regretted how often she had allowed herself to be ignored and disrespected by family members at holiday gatherings. She was humiliated every time, sometimes openly, sometimes known only to her. She despaired that she could never assert her need to be treated with respect. She was so disappointed by repeatedly being tortured when she could be experiencing the joy of these events with people who treated her respectfully. She was distressed by feelings of regret. She considered whether her regrets were valid. She reflected on her desire to be treated with respect and love. Lisette decided that it was time to be assertive, and to let her family know that they needed to treat her better. If they refused, she'd consider not attending their gatherings.*

Circle one. My regret is:

*Excessive* *Healthy*

Write out one part of the regret you are experiencing. Try framing it as a "What if?" question or an "If only" scenario.

______________________________________________________________

______________________________________________________________

______________________________________________________________

______________________________________________________________

______________________________________________________________

If you could have the experience again, what would you do?

___

___

___

If you could help prevent others going through that scenario, what would you do?

___

___

___

If you are experiencing healthy regret, what have you learned as a result?

___

___

___

Does your regret reveal something important to you about what you value in life?

___

___

___

How might you be able to assist others with what you have learned?

___

___

___

## *Self-Blame*

Blame is allocating responsibility. It involves shifting responsibility from one thing to another. Self-blame happens when you shift responsibility toward yourself. This may or may not be called for, or useful. Self-blame can be useful when, within the experience of remorse and regret, it is an adaptive response of taking responsibility where there is a clear need to do so.

**Excessive self-blame:** Instead of allocating responsibility correctly, self-blame can lead you to take on excessive responsibility and judge yourself harshly as a result. When excessive, self-blame can narrow your perspective, capability, and capacity to act. It becomes toxic when unnecessary. Catastrophic life events and overwhelming chaos may lead you to blame yourself in order to feel you have some measure of control. Self-blame may be the only way to respond to disastrous, uncontrollable life events. For example, if you are caught up in a random assault while out with friends, you may blame yourself for being in the wrong place at the wrong time. A child may blame themself for their parents' divorce. Someone may blame themself for a best friend's unexpected suicide. Such self-blame can provide a focus and direction for overwhelming, chaotic thoughts, emotions, and other internal sensations. It can be unrelenting, unresolvable, and unanswerable.

**Healthy self-blame:** A healthy acceptance of responsibility may provide a pathway for engaging in appropriate remorse and regret. Understanding your role in something that has gone wrong gives you a pathway to respond appropriately and effectively. Your responses might include righting a wrong, apologizing, or seeking help.

> *For many years, Malcolm experienced crushing self-blame for his father's suicide. He had left his father alone and in deep distress. He had been a teenager at the time. With help, Malcolm realized he wouldn't blame any other teenager for the self-inflicted death of an adult—much less an adult who should have been responsible for Malcolm's welfare. Malcolm's perspective began to shift, as he started thinking of his teenage self with sadness. He had experienced so much pain as a result of his father's depression. So he offered that younger part of himself more grace and understanding, and considered how others could learn from what he went through.*

If you are experiencing excessive self-blame, consider the right proportion of blame to allocate to various parties.

Why you are to blame: ______________________________

______________________________

______________________________

______________________________

What others are responsible for: ______________________________

______________________________

______________________________

______________________________

What was up to chance or forces outside your control: ______________________________

______________________________

______________________________

Write about what you are truly responsible for: ______________________________

______________________________

______________________________

______________________________

Is it possible to take action to remedy, heal, or repair the things you take responsibility for? What might you do?

________________________________________

________________________________________

________________________________________

________________________________________

If you are experiencing healthy self-blame, is there anything you need to do to fulfill your responsibility, take action, or integrate this lesson?

________________________________________

________________________________________

________________________________________

________________________________________

## *Guilt*

Guilt provides you with a declaration that someone (at times yourself) has done something wrong. Guilt may be used to address the behaviors associated with wrongdoing. Guilt allows you to examine the function of behavior that caused the wrongdoing or distress. However, guilt that becomes associated with harsh judgment and condemnation can transfix you and lead you to be stuck.

**Excessive guilt:** If guilt does transfix you in one perspective or glue you to one spot, it can become toxic and paralyzing. Guilt can make you vulnerable to manipulation. Others may leverage it to gain influence over you, taking you further into inaction or wrong action. Feeling guilty can also excuse you from taking right action, which weakens you. For example, making a business mistake may provide you with a reason for never taking a risk again. Guilt can reduce you, bring you down to size, and put you in a box.

**Healthy guilt:** When well applied, guilt allows you to effectively name the problem that caused your distress. Guilt allows you to pinpoint exactly what went wrong. It then provides a focus for a healthy sense of responsibility. It clarifies your regrets and sources of remorse. Guilt points to the action you must take to repair damage, or the line in the sand you must draw and not cross again. As you learn from past mistakes, guilt makes it possible to start again, take new action, and repair yourself.

*Madelyn spent years wrapped in guilt about being dissatisfied with her marriage. She sank into a deep pit of despair over the thought of ending the relationship. She felt guilty about her own failure. She felt guilty about not meeting cultural expectations. She felt guilty of destroying a stable two-parent home for her daughters. She felt crippled. Then she wrote about the story of her marriage in her journal, and read it. A sense of distance from that guilt arose. She realized that if any of her friends went through this, she would be encouraging them to end the marriage. So why am I torturing myself? she wondered. Madelyn knew she valued a partnership with someone who respected her, and her husband showed no respect, concern, or kindness. Plus, a dysfunctional family was good for neither her daughters nor her. She decided to shake off the paralysis caused by guilt and start feeling good about her desire to seek a divorce.*

If you are experiencing excessive guilt, write about what or who is broken.

_______________________________________________

_______________________________________________

_______________________________________________

_______________________________________________

_______________________________________________

Is there is anything that can be done to repair what is broken? If so, write it down. If not, write about any alternative actions you can take to ease guilt, change the situation, or even leave a toxic circumstance.

______________________________________________

______________________________________________

______________________________________________

How might you prevent this from happening again in your life or others' lives?

______________________________________________

______________________________________________

______________________________________________

If your guilt is healthy, what is the lesson that you can reflect on or teach others?

______________________________________________

______________________________________________

______________________________________________

## *Shame*

Whereas guilt refers to feeling bad about an action, shame refers to feeling bad about yourself. If you have a chronic sense of shame, you feel broken, inherently bad, unfixable, unworthy. This sense of brokenness disconnects you from society, and also from yourself. Shame creates multiple barriers: to your past, your present, and your future sense of self.

**Excessive shame:** Shame damages your perspective on your worth. Doubt about your worth is a crippling cause of procrastination. It may lead you to feel frozen, unable to act, choose, or find direction. Through this sense of unworthiness, shame both undermines and disconnects you from your values. This disconnection heightens uncertainty about your contribution to the world. A deep and abiding sense of shame is a key factor behind substance abuse and other excessive behaviors that don't work. Shame may transport you anywhere but being present with your pain. The internal critic is at its worst when shame is at its deepest. Experiences of remorse, regret, self-blame, and guilt may be supercharged by shame. In this state, you may focus on scripts, such as "once broken, always broken" or "I am damaged goods, wanted by no one, only fit to be discarded."

**Healthy shame:** The gift of shame is having a sense of limits. Without it, you would have no caution in your actions. Shame can be a reality check on the sense that all will go on as it is forever, but things do change and loss does happen. Shame demonstrates your limitations, highlights your natural dependence on and interdependence with others, and reveals a humility that is useful within the reality of life experience. These limitations demonstrate the need for respectful relationships with others, respect for the environments you are in, gratitude for the things that help you live an uncertain life in a fragile environment, and ongoing awareness that life is extremely short and involves chaos and unpredictability. A sense of healthy shame may encourage you to gain extra skills, education, or physical ability, or to undertake any training program that will help you master something. Shame may offer motivation for teaching others to change and improve, it may cause you to act, and it may be an opportunity for self-examination at its deepest point—focusing on what you need to work on most. In that focus, there is hope of informing your life's meaning and purpose. You can work with what is broken to create what you value in your life. Shame is therefore a pathway to rediscovering your values and acting in ways that reflect your true worth.

*Charlize reflected on her deep sense of shame. She felt that, at her core, something was not right with her. The destructive addictions in her family had to be kept secret in order to protect the family from public shame. As a result, she took on that sense of shame. She hated the secret that was no secret to her. It caused her to believe that she was flawed, potentially an addict herself if she ever let substances into her life. Her experience of chronic pain, and the battle to avoid prescription opioids, all piled up as evidence that she was truly broken. But whenever she told her story to trusted friends, she could glimpse that the fault was not entirely hers.*

*Once Charlize could offer herself a compassionate perspective, she realized she could face what was broken: her addicted relatives, her family's attitudes, and her own body. Among those, she could change one thing. Charlize could do something about her body by seeking the surgical assistance she needed.*

If you are experiencing excessive shame, write about what you believe is broken about you.

______________________________________________

______________________________________________

______________________________________________

______________________________________________

______________________________________________

______________________________________________

Is there an opportunity to engage in some form of restoration, using your skills in compassion and acceptance? Write down what you might do to help yourself.

______________________________________________

______________________________________________

______________________________________________

If your shame is healthy, what is it prompting you to do? In what way do you feel motivated to learn, change, or grow?

______________________________________________

______________________________________________

______________________________________________

## *Self-Hatred and Self-Rejection*

Along with your shame, you may also be positioning yourself as an object of your hatred. The harsh inner critic may reveal itself in actual speech. Brené Brown (2015) describes this speech as the "bathroom voice." Others call it a "lizard voice" that rises up to make the most vile and base accusations and judgments. It is the critic that pounces on you at two o'clock in the morning when you wake up in a cold sweat.

**Excessive self-hatred and self-rejection:** You may be experiencing an overwhelming concoction of emotions caused by pain. By hating yourself, you are totally rejecting your own self, your actions, and your worth. Self-hatred may cause self-harm, self-punishment, and self-mortification through actions that are both ritualistic and spontaneous. The never-ending spinning of thoughts may cause nauseating distress, which can be both a symptom and a cause that reinforces virulent self-hatred. You may feel a need to cut or harm yourself in order to stop such cycles. Your existential pain can feel relieved in the presence of real pain and bodily consequences. Otherwise, you fear being left with an overwhelming sense of shame and humiliation.

**Healthy self-hatred and self-rejection:** It may surprise you to think that self-hatred can be healthy. If you treat the experience with openness, interest, and curiosity, you can make a place for a compassionate response. All emotions that we experience are "normal." That is, your emotions erupt out of your experience of being human. These emotions provide us with signals. Self-hatred can be a signal that something in you needs your attention. What is it that you hate so much? What about yourself are you rejecting? The answers can be a useful guide to exploring your distress. With a compassionate response, you can then work with those causes of pain.

*Lani was caught up in how much she hated herself for making such bad decisions in her life. She hated that she was different, that she did not fit in, that she didn't look like anyone around her, that she chose unusual careers, that her family was different, that her husband was a risky choice. It was always something different. Why couldn't she just fit in? Be normal? Be satisfied? She could just scream.*

*With a compassionate lens, Lani first made a list of all the things she hated about herself. Then she wrote the story behind each one with open curiosity. It turned out there were reasons why she felt so different, why she made the choices she did, and why she continued to work in such a demanding field. She treated each item on the list with respect. They all had drawbacks and they all had benefits. By holding herself with respect, Lani began to realize there was dignity in being different and courageous. As she gained kinder new perspectives on herself, she found that her sense of meaning in her life increased.*

If you are experiencing excessive self-hatred and self-rejection, identify the parts of yourself that are the focus of this emotion.

What you hate about yourself: ____________________________________________

____________________________________________

____________________________________________

____________________________________________

____________________________________________

Now treat each part you hate about yourself as you would a friend having a similar experience. Write about it kindly, telling the story behind it, and being curious about what this part of yourself has to say.

____________________________________________

____________________________________________

____________________________________________

____________________________________________

If your self-hatred is healthy, write down the lessons learned and describe the ways you now respond so you can keep working toward your preferred life outcomes.

____________________________________________

____________________________________________

____________________________________________

____________________________________________

____________________________________________

## *Self-Disgust and Self-Loathing*

When you are disgusted by yourself or loathe yourself, feelings of rejection get more intense. Self-disgust and self-loathing are emotions closely associated with autonomic, or natural, responses like vomiting and excreting bodily waste. When you are an object of your own disgust, you are revolted by your own being. Such disgust may have a cascading effect that can lead to physical nausea, self-medicating your pain and distress, and even possible self-destruction. The body of research indicates that self-rejection, self-hatred, self-loathing, and self-disgust may provide insight into excessive behaviors that can decrease length of life. These behaviors include experiences of drug addiction, risk taking, poorly regulated sexual activity, and unsafe sex. Use of alcohol, cigarettes, and illicit substances are all likely to increase in the presence of these toxic emotions.

**Excessive self-disgust and self-loathing:** These responses come with a high price, as you may reach a point where you treat yourself destructively. Believing yourself to be unacceptable, disgusting, or revolting underpins a belief that you are a threat to society, others, and your own well-being. Such experiences can lead to a variety of self-harming and suicidal responses. You can find relief by seeking therapeutic help immediately, as you may be at risk. Professionals are trained to help you. If you see yourself here, please put down this book and reach out to one.

**Healthy self-disgust and self-loathing:** Once again, how can this be healthy? Anyone can experience major life setbacks that take them to places they do not want to be. Severe medical conditions can change your sense of self. Sudden poverty or homelessness can be devastating. Experiencing overwhelming trauma, death, destruction, and disasters can expose you to a sense of self-loathing for witnessing or surviving the event. You may have been rejected or betrayed by someone you love. Each of these experiences can raise emotions of disgust and loathing that you direct toward yourself. If you treat these experiences with compassion, you can develop different, healthier perspectives. A stance of open interest and curiosity can inspire useful responses to the transforming life events you have experienced.

*Charlize felt she was sinking to the bottom of a well, with no end in sight and no way out. She loathed herself for being so weak, confused, and distressed about her pain. Memories of family chaos made her feel dirty and disgusting. Her dysfunctional family had convinced her no one would ever want her. She felt there was no point going on.*

*A friend randomly called, realized how distressed Charlize was, and came over to Charlize's house immediately. This friend's arrival interrupted her plans. After a good night's sleep, Charlize found she could focus on the one thing that she could actually change. She needed to schedule her operation to deal with the pain that made her deeply uncomfortable in her own body. The next morning, her friend handed her the phone, and Charlize called the surgeon's office.*

If you are experiencing excessive self-disgust and self-loathing, you may need the compassionate lens of a health professional. With them, you can identify what is making you feel so sickened at heart. With kindness, start becoming curious about what your disgust and loathing want you to know about your pain. Write whatever comes to mind.

___

___

___

___

___

When these thoughts of revulsion arise, write down three things you can compassionately do to help yourself.

1. ___
2. ___
3. ___

If your self-disgust and self-loathing has helped you learn something, write it down.

___

___

___

___

___

How might you assist others who are challenged by these self-punishing emotions?

________________________________________________________________________

________________________________________________________________________

________________________________________________________________________

________________________________________________________________________

## Compassion Transforms Suffering

This range of responses to pain can shape and inform your life. By approaching these responses with a compassionate lens, you gain transformative skills that are vital to the process of self-forgiveness. A compassionate lens allows you to examine events in your life more openly and flexibly, as well as your responses to them. New perspectives result that can help you reinterpret and reframe your story. Applying this skill is how you transform a toxic response to suffering. Compassion helps you reinterpret and respond to your inner critic. When you are in states that feel frozen, a compassionate lens can bring the warmth of new perspectives for taking action and choosing your life's direction.

Just as a wound must be opened up and cleaned out before it can heal, you must get through your unhealthy responses to life so you can open up with compassion and heal from the inside out. Your pain, and the toxic responses you have adopted to cover it, are actually pointing you to go deeper. The deep work of self-forgiveness requires inquiry, curiosity, and open examination of your hurt with a compassionate lens. This work transforms experiences of failure, loss, and rejection into the ability to clarify what you are really seeking.

In our universe, there is infinitely more that is unknown than known. In the unknown is danger and chaos—and also creativity and opportunity. The skills you are practicing will allow you to conjure what you value from the unknown. By being willing to make mistakes and use a compassionate lens to reflect, you can advance by trial and error.

Reflecting on this chapter, what has resonated with you?

________________________________________________________________________________

________________________________________________________________________________

________________________________________________________________________________

________________________________________________________________________________

Is there a story you need to tell in order to transform it? Consider writing it down.

________________________________________________________________________________

________________________________________________________________________________

________________________________________________________________________________

________________________________________________________________________________

________________________________________________________________________________

Is there a particular area, or part of yourself, you want to focus on as you move to the next chapter?

________________________________________________________________________________

________________________________________________________________________________

________________________________________________________________________________

________________________________________________________________________________

________________________________________________________________________________

To find what you seek on your momentous life journey, you must enter the chaos of the unknown. By being willing to fail, able to learn, and eager to grow from experience, you can chart a pathway in that unknown. Repeatedly absorbing and transforming pain and distress, discomfort and heartache, becomes the price of discovering how to learn despite chaos. When you forgive yourself, you build a reserve of strength to draw on.

CHAPTER 3

# Shift Old Beliefs Through New Perspectives

When you stand outdoors in a dark place free of artificial light, you are able to see the vastness of the night sky. Billions of points of light adorn it. Similarly, when you visit a high place on a clear day, you see views revealing a vast landscape that encompasses infinite detail. As you take in the sights from these places, you experience wonder beyond conscious understanding. This wonder reveals your expansive sense of self as a container for all the life you have lived, the life you have yet to live, and all the possibilities for your future. Moments like this show us the power of perspective. You have a self that is expansive and takes in a sense of the limitless.

By trying on a compassionate lens in the last chapter, you were also practicing the skill of taking new perspectives. This skill helps you more deeply examine your story, revealing your truth that you need to respond to. In this chapter, I invite you to widen your ability to explore and deepen this sense of perspective. These are skills you already use in many areas of your life. Here, you will leverage them to shift old beliefs about those stories you have been keeping too close. Then you can explore options that allow you to heal and strengthen. New perspectives on the old stories you've told yourself repeatedly can open you up to pursue your most authentic life.

## The Three Aspects of Self

Our perspective can be broken into three broad aspects of self: expansive self, story self, and functional self (Hayes, Barnes-Holmes, and Roche 2001). First, as I already shared, we have space to develop ever more complex representations of who we are. We are often not aware of our *expansive self*. This is the self that gently holds and notices all you experience, and all the possibilities of that experience. Whatever your age or life experience, you have been you for your whole life. This is the self that has always been, is now, and will always be—a sense of being eternally present. It is the you that notices, dreams, and thinks, to the edge of the universe and beyond, to the beginning of time and before. This self holds all the life you can imagine, experience, and engage. It contains any number of events, whether it wants to or not.

Another self, the *story self*, contains and responds to the many stories that define you to yourself and to others, as a child, student, sibling, partner, lover, hater, parent, achiever, failure, career person, worker, hobbyist, and a billion other possibilities. This self is a shape-shifter, a chameleon, a role, a mask facilitating your flexibility to face life and all its roles. It fills important and unimportant overlapping and sometimes conflicting roles. This self is something you can choose to be or to change from one story to another. Life may take away some roles through aging, shift in status, loss, injury, death, success, failure, and many other ways. The story self is represented as the content of all that you experience in life. Each of these experiences may impact you immediately, gradually, or imperceptibly, changing this sense of self.

Then there is the self that undertakes all the functions of living. This *functional self* constantly interacts with both what is happening around you and what is happening within you. It takes into account your history and expectations. This self functions as a physical, thinking, emotional, sensing, social, and interactive being. It is the self that breathes, moves, feels, and responds to its environment and circumstances. Built by the revealing mystery that is your DNA, it can run totally on automatic in so many areas, such as breathing, digestion, a range of sensations, many emotions, and so on. And yet in so many ways this self is responsive to your wants, appetites, desires, thoughts, and needs.

The functional self is where automatic responses happen. These automatic responses are really useful in many ways. Once you learn how to do complex things, they help you type, drive, ride a bike, and wash dishes while talking to someone. But also, a loud crash might cause you to automatically jump, look, or shift. This response can be lifesaving. It can also be embarrassing or shaming if it is out of proportion to the event. For those who survive traumatic events, this experience is frequent. If a truck backfires in traffic, a military veteran might dive to the pavement. Automatic responses can help you survive in some circumstances and distress you deeply in others, which is a problem when a range of perceived threats cause disproportionate fight-flight-or-freeze responses. Your consciousness is grappling with the biological and social self, as well as limitations on how much your consciousness can control the functional part of you.

*Charlize grappled with her automatic responses to the smell of alcohol on someone's breath. She loved to socialize with good friends and preferred to stick to soda water or nonalcoholic drinks. When her friends drank alcohol, Charlize automatically felt a sense of sickness in her stomach and wanted to get away from them, despite enjoying their company. She felt annoyed with herself and then distressed by the cause of her discomfort: an automatic response caused by years of witnessing excessive alcohol use by her family members.*

Charlize's expansive self was holding space for the information about how being around people who were drinking affected her, and was observing her responses. Her story self was reminding her that alcohol has impacted her life course and that it affects her deeply. Her functional self was in automatic mode trying to protect her.

Let's explore your experience of the expansive self, the story self, and the functional self. Think of any time when an automatic response tried to override your preference to have an experience. Allow your reflection to reveal the richness of the information you might gain from this discovery. Your reflection can result in new perspectives that inform healing, restoration, renewal, and discovery. Here's an example.

> *Lisette had to board a crowded international flight for a vacation. Her functional self felt claustrophobic and nervous, and she had a strong urge to just go home. She had memories of the time she was trying to get into a big game at a stadium and got caught in the crush of a large crowd. Her story self was telling her* "I feel really distressed in any crowd." *She knew that if she concentrated on the feeling that story created—the increasing nausea—she probably would not get on that flight. Her expansive self reminded her that it is okay to be aware of safety in crowds. She stepped back and got out of the initial rush, and waited until the line thinned out. Then Lisette was able to board the plane more confidently.*

Now look at how this has played out in your experience.

What was it you wanted to do?

______________________________________________________________________

What was an automatic response that occurred, which might have drawn you away from what you wanted?

______________________________________________________________________

______________________________________________________________________

______________________________________________________________________

What was the story you were telling yourself?

_______________________________________________

_______________________________________________

_______________________________________________

_______________________________________________

_______________________________________________

How could you have had, or did you have, an expansive perspective of this event?

_______________________________________________

_______________________________________________

_______________________________________________

_______________________________________________

What are your reflections?

_______________________________________________

_______________________________________________

_______________________________________________

_______________________________________________

_______________________________________________

Let's deepen your ability to make room for your experiences. Doing this next meditation can help you take flexible action that allows you to do what is important, and live a life that works.

# A Meditation on Three Forms of Self

This is a breathing exercise. Get into a comfortable position: you may lie down, sit, or take any position in which you are able to focus on this exercise. Please stop at any time if you feel discomfort. You can close your eyes and listen to an audio version by visiting http://www.newharbinger.com/45694.

> First, bring your attention to your breathing. Concentrate on following your breath in and out of your body—do this for four or five breaths.
>
> If you find your thoughts drifting, bring your attention gently back to your breath, and then resume following the instructions.
>
> Choose a time of life when you were quite young, and doing something where you were breathing hard. Find any story in your life. Perhaps it was an experience of running in a playground. Just observe how that child was breathing. Take some time to immerse your attention in that experience.
>
> Now consider your self at another stage of life, perhaps your teens, running for a school bus because you were late. Or maybe you were playing team sports. Whatever is an experience that is memorable for you. Take some time to immerse your attention in that experience.
>
> Once more, consider yourself as an adult. Choose any story from your life where your breathing is noticeable: dancing with a friend, or being nervous at a job interview, or doing some strenuous gardening. Take some time to immerse your attention in that experience.
>
> Notice how your breath has served you to engage in life in different circumstances.
>
> Now just return to focusing on your breath here and now. Take some time to immerse your attention in that experience.

Well done. Now let's reflect on the rich information revealed by the experiences you have just observed. Please write about your expansive experience of following your breathing across your life span, and being present in all those experiences.

_______________________________________________

_______________________________________________

_______________________________________________

_______________________________________________

_______________________________________________

In what ways can you connect with a variety of experiences of your story self: as a child, a teen, an adult, and as you are here and now? (Perhaps you recall experiencing a sunny day, smelling a flower, meeting a good friend.)

_______________________________________________

_______________________________________________

_______________________________________________

_______________________________________________

_______________________________________________

What are your reflections on following your continuous experience of breathing as a function in your life?

_______________________________________________

_______________________________________________

_______________________________________________

_______________________________________________

_______________________________________________

As you can see, you can observe yourself. It can be challenging to create and hold a space of transcendent experience for you to consciously and willingly engage the work that needs to be done. But it truly is simple, as you just demonstrated in the following ways:

- You observe and you can observe that you are observing. This is how you gain perspective through your expansive self.
- By contacting versions of yourself that no longer exist, that are in your past, you gain perspective from your story self.
- Observing your breathing is observing your experience as a functional self.

During whatever experience you have in life, when you start to notice that experience, you can observe the you that is noticing. We will refer to this exercise and apply it in different forms throughout this journey of self-forgiveness. It will help you expand your ability to take on new perspectives and is an important skill for your journey within.

Your capacity to notice allows the development of multiple perspectives on any experience and any resulting story you tell yourself. Through suspending harsh, critical judgment, your expansive self can take any perspective it wants on actual and imagined events. This self can then step outside that experience and, with openness, interest, and curiosity, find the pathway that works for you. In this workbook, you will be given the opportunity to call on these concepts and develop practical applications that suit your needs. I encourage you to work through the exercises in this chapter to unpack old beliefs and open new possibilities. Let's look at how doing this work helped Lisette.

> *Lisette felt terrible about upcoming holiday celebrations with her family. She realized that she was blaming herself for feeling bad—telling herself to just get over it. To practice perspective-taking skills, she took some time to meditate on feeling terrible about holidays. She allowed herself to be open, interested, and curious about her experience. She stopped judging herself and took a stance that feeling terrible was neither good nor bad. Instead, it was something to be observed with a compassionate lens from a different perspective.*
>
> *First, she explored her experience of her functional self, asking:* Where do I feel terrible? *There were sensations of her skin crawling, feeling sweaty, and her heart racing. With compassion, she asked her body to put that feeling into words:* I hate being used up and then ignored by my relatives. *Lisette made room for this response and held it with compassion.*

*Then she looked at her story self, recalling a number of holidays, times when others were given expensive gifts and she was given some bars of soap, when others were praised for how appreciated they were and her efforts went unacknowledged, and how on each of these occasions she had shrugged off her disappointment because she blamed herself for not being good enough. She held these memories with an open, curious awareness.*

*Finally, she used her expansive perspective to wonder if she might be good enough. She began viewing herself as someone worthy of compassion and better treatment. She realized there were important lessons to be learned about who she listened to and how she spent her energy. Maybe she could even see beyond her family's limitations on her.*

In your life experience, you can start to practice this form of noticing. You can notice that you have space for all the experiences of your life, both real and imagined. You are more than your stories; you are more than the functions of living. In that space of possibility, you have infinite capacity to develop new stories to engage with and to direct your functional self toward. Growth and possibility are revealed by your perspective.

Be forewarned: There is a paradox to this level of change. On one hand, this experience of expansion that you will practice is the foundation for a powerful creative imagination. This is the imagination that can change the world and create the future in all its innovation and invention. Hypatia of Alexandria, Leonardo Da Vinci, Marie Curie, and Nikola Tesla are great examples of how imagination can foreshadow the future. Vision creates new perspectives in art, culture, science, and engineering that then create powerful concepts to open a new world. This is all possible for you. On the other hand, I want to acknowledge that new possibilities can be threatening. Anything new may challenge and sometimes sweep away the old. This can bring unexpected consequences, sometimes regret, for not doing something beneficial sooner, or regret for that which is lost in the midst of change. In this journey, self-forgiveness is founded on your values. Using the foundation of your values will help you face the paradox of change that you are likely to experience on your journey of discovery.

## Perspective Taking as a Lever

Like physical tools, psychological tools are only useful when put into action with intention. A lever is neutral until it is put to use with an intention. It may be used to open or close, to lift or pull down, constructively or destructively. The same can be said for your perspective.

Therefore, it is important to set your intention to align with what you truly value, what you hold to be worthy. Then you can practice and build skills that are useful. And break apart, recycle, and rebuild what is not currently working.

In using perspective taking as a lever, you will be practicing a form of mindfulness. You will be bringing your attention to a specific point, or task, with intention and presence, which allows you to notice and engage with internal events (thoughts, emotions, images, physical sensations) and respond effectively. With inner flexibility and agility, you will be better able to handle external events that impact you in some way.

Victor Frankl was a survivor of the Nazi death camps. He identified that the ability to notice created the space between the stimulus of external experience and internal response. He noted that, despite the unpredictable physical and mental cruelty inflected upon him and millions of others, he always had the ability to notice and become aware of what was most valuable in his life. This was true for others also. He helped them create an internal space that made it possible for them to choose how to respond. This choice allowed him, and those going through the camps with him, to face both death and life with a chosen perspective that could not be taken from them (Frankl 1985).

As you notice events, they may be externally and objectively "real." Or they can be subjectively and imaginatively, vibrantly, and powerfully "real." In either case, your expansive self can stand back from this range of events to observe them. In this place of detached observation, you will find the space to create choice. The power described by Frankl was the choice of how to respond. This choice to respond can then be informed by the full range of your values and possible actions. The following story shows how this works.

*Fourteen-year-old Gerard was dirty, tired, and in pain. He had fallen off his bike as a truck came close to him. He had landed hard, and something felt strange in his leg. The bike frame had broken and cut his leg badly. Then there was a tumble of events: an ambulance, emergency admission, the loss of his bike, the pain. Everything felt like it was going sideways. He was becoming physically ill with the anxiety he felt at what his family would say. A nurse noticed that he was really pale. She took his pulse and other vital signs, and she talked to him with acceptance and reassurance. "We are going to patch you up, you will get antibiotics, and the main thing is you are alive. You could have gone under that truck but you didn't. You are alive. You are going to be okay, and your family will be glad you are okay." Her kind tone and reassurance gave Gerard a new perspective. His accident was not the end of the world. A bike could be replaced, his life couldn't, and his health was going to eventually return.*

Gerard's functional self is at the fore: his need to survive a serious accident, to begin healing. But very quickly his story self took over, telling him the story of being in trouble, things going sideways, losing the bike, being a nuisance. It was only when the nurse spoke to him with compassion that his expansive self was reminded of the bigger picture. This perspective, that his life and health were of greater importance than the story of "things going sideways," was the one that brought a shift toward healing. Gerard was able to move from the story to a broader view. While the functional issues of health and repair were important, these things would pass, and a greater experience of life awaited him. This broader perspective was also part of his healing process.

Now it's your turn to try this shift. Consider a story in your life when you were in trouble. Write what that story was, without judging if it is right or wrong. Try to capture what it was like to be in trouble.

_______________________________________________

_______________________________________________

_______________________________________________

_______________________________________________

_______________________________________________

_______________________________________________

_______________________________________________

What are the thoughts, feelings, and sensations you recall as you write down this story?

_______________________________________________

_______________________________________________

_______________________________________________

_______________________________________________

_______________________________________________

With openness, interest, and curiosity, examine that story. Consider what other perspectives might have been helpful for you to adopt.

If you were reading this story for the first time as a close friend of someone in trouble, what perspective could you bring? Identify the perspective shift that might help your friend who is struggling. Then write down this perspective, as a good friend to that person.

Take a deep breath to connect with your expansive self. Write about how your expansive self observes this story.

Think about how your memories influenced your experience. What stories from your past are revealed to you?

Are there any aspects of your functional self that seem fixed in their responses but could change with a different perspective? If so, observe and write about your choices.

Is there another way to tell this story? Write down another view of the story as you respond to these new perspectives.

In this exercise you have used perspective as a lever. You have begun to expand your perspective by noticing. Now let's draw on your sense of monsters from chapter 1. When you are observing this situation and story, do any of the following show up? Circle any monsters you recognize.

| | |
|---|---|
| *the voice of the inner critic* | *the voice of the impostor* |
| *the voice of fear* | *the fear of failure* |
| *the fear of success* | *the voice of doubt* |

These monsters lie within the darkest experiences of your life; yet each of these experiences contains or tries to hide a transformative truth. To gain the perspective you need for this truth discovery, you must learn to observe your monsters and what they hold, protect, or conceal. Within the darkness and mystery of your experience, a light waits to be uncovered. Observing with exploration and curiosity develops your ability to transform this internal conversation through perspective taking. Perspective taking allows you to reveal and examine the answer that is within you. Perspective taking is a skill that allows you to pass through your fear...and *do what you want, be what you want.*

Consider the story of Lisette. Her monster is her inner critic, who is always telling her that she is not good enough. When it came up about holidays with her family, by using her skills to observe her functional, story, and expansive selves, she found her values and the truth of her need for respect, recognition, and self-compassion. Now let's apply this to the monster you have circled.

Name the monster and tell its story. When did you first encounter that monster? Under what circumstances does it show itself? What does it say to you?

______________________________________________________________________

______________________________________________________________________

______________________________________________________________________

______________________________________________________________________

______________________________________________________________________

______________________________________________________________________

Using the skills you have been practicing so far, go into a spacious state of mind. You might do a breathing exercise, write out another side to the story, or take a deep breath before reading what you just wrote. How can you give your experience room?

_______________________________________________

_______________________________________________

_______________________________________________

_______________________________________________

What in your story is hidden, concealed, protected, or withheld?

_______________________________________________

_______________________________________________

_______________________________________________

_______________________________________________

What in your story is pointing to the transformative truth within you?

_______________________________________________

_______________________________________________

_______________________________________________

_______________________________________________

_______________________________________________

Well done! You have just practiced a transformation. Now we will explore some more skills in greater depth. These are skills you will be able to call on throughout your life.

# Finding Perspectives That Help

It's true: there are an infinite number of ways that we can look at something. However, within the context of your life, there are only a few ways that that work, giving us the mental and emotional freedom we are seeking. Three important questions inform perspective taking that works (Villatte, Villatte, and Hayes 2016).

*Does this perspective help fit things together in a way that works or is coherent?*

Your perspective needs to be informed by the ability to make a meaningful whole of the information you are observing. Does what you are perceiving make sense? Is it believable, and do your conclusions regarding these perceptions hang together? From this place of understanding, you can make decisions that help you navigate life.

*Does the way I view this experience take into account its context in a way that is sensitive to what is happening?*

By sensitively considering what is happening in and around the event, and what is contributing to it, you allow your expansive self to observe and help. This builds your ability to put things into context. You can ask further questions like: What is really going on here (function)? What has contributed to this event (story)? Does this perspective fit with this context (expansion)? Is this perspective both real and true, given the context, or am I creating a story around this perspective that is an assumption (or not necessarily true)?

*Does this perspective allow me to increase my flexibility to respond to what life brings next?*

A useful perspective is one that allows you to look at the broader picture, to see the whole of what you are observing. Taking perspective ensures that your response fits into the context of your experience, and is flexible and adaptable. These flexible responses—or *psychological flexibility*—give you the skills to navigate difficult, unpredictable circumstances. You can then choose the right level of support and the right level of capacity you need to flexibly meet the challenges you face on a daily basis.

Reflecting on these three questions can help narrow down your possible responses to life events. These questions are like a three-legged stool, each supporting the other to form a stable platform of support for important decisions. They form the basis for any choice, so here is a worksheet you can fill out any time you want to ensure your perspective will support a beneficial choice. You can download it for repeated use at http://www.newharbinger.com/45694.

The decision I need to make: ______________________________

______________________________

______________________________

______________________________

______________________________

My perspective on the situation: ______________________________

______________________________

______________________________

______________________________

This perspective makes sense because: ______________________________

______________________________

______________________________

______________________________

If it doesn't make sense, try taking a different perspective.

This perspective takes the following context into consideration: ______________________________

______________________________

______________________________

______________________________

If there are aspects of the situation you have not considered, try taking a different perspective.

If this perspective traps you in a way of thinking, feeling, or acting, and you don't know what you will do if things go differently from how you expect, try taking a different perspective.

# Language Is Sticky

Warning: you are about to take a shallow dive into the messy history and strange properties of language. I promise it will be worth it. Why? Because at the end of this section, you will be able to develop more skills that free up your perspective taking. You will be less judgmental about why, or how, you have developed certain ways of looking at things, and more able to drop those judgments. This greater sense of open interest and curiosity is the key to developing new perspectives.

Consider this sentence: A *cat can be a fluff ball, a fluff ball can be a* ______________. Most likely, you would say "cat." Yet you could have also said many other correct things, like "nuisance," "danger," or "soft toy." But now cat and fluff ball are linked in your mind in a two-way connection, whether it makes sense or not.

Your memory is always adding new meaning through identification and interpretation of language. Language creates connections, and these connections, or links, stick. Unless you suffer an injury, these links create memory. Therefore, the connections continue to stick. Brain experiments show that we never forget what is taken in; it is just that the more practiced the recall, the easier the recall.

This stickiness of human language affects your perspective taking. Sometimes, when your perception is primed and influenced by these language connections, you see what you expect to see and not what is actually there. Or you will see things in a certain way—until that paradigm is interrupted.

To interrupt this sticky learning, remind yourself to be open, interested, and curious about things and circumstances as well as the way you perceive them. This openness is a foundation for making useful and expansive inquiries about your experience. As you have been learning throughout this workbook, when you drop harsh critical judgments, and replace them with compassionate acceptance, new possibilities arise. Acceptance allows you to see through new lenses (compassion is one of many powerful examples) that may help you see situations and circumstances from more than one point of view.

The power of story that you began working with in chapter 1 shows how deep this sticky learning can be. This power of learning through connection arises because your human ability to think as you do is unique. The exercise of *a fluff ball can be…* is something only a human has capacity for; it is automatic for us and does not need to be taught. However, this simple process of two-way connection is incredibly powerful, and the basis of the way human intelligence has exploded across the planet. Your ability to learn through connection builds incredibly complex webs of understanding about all you perceive. That is why consciously building skills in perspective taking is so important: it allows you to respond flexibly to what you face in life (Villatte and Villatte 2013).

As a baby, you learned to respond instantly to a variety of stimuli, in a way that allowed you to have your needs met: food, comfort, cleanliness, contact. From that arose your sense of your three levels of self. Each level is necessary in learning about, responding to, and changing your world. For example, you were hungry (functional self); you indicated to someone who cared for you that you needed food (this is expansion, as you were aware *they* were not *you* and needed to understand your needs); they fed you with a smile (now a story might develop about how you asked for food and got a loving response). Through everyday interactions, you became aware of how your communication, and even your presence, affected people around you. Consider the complexity of this simple interaction: you spoke to someone, they turned to you and smiled and responded.

Layers and layers of learning come from simple interactions—like talking, connection, pleasure, and response—that all become connected on many levels. We will continue to explore this, using examples to illustrate how you can use this power of communication and attention in a way that helps you build the life you deserve.

Your ability to reflect on your inner experience is foundational to your sense of self. And just like the biblical story of Eden, this expanding realization of self involves a loss of innocence within yourself. It is also the genesis of the inner critic and the birthplace of monsters. The loss of innocence arises from the process of differentiating between yes and no, right and wrong, and eventually good and evil.

You learn, very early in life, that you have a sense of "I"—the self that experiences all events. However, you also have a sense of "me"—the object to which events happen. Consider the statement: "I am not myself today." Who is the "myself" that I am not today, relative to any other day? This differentiation between "I" and "me/myself" is a product of human language. Remember, language is a basic tool of human development through learning, connection, and communication of insights across space and time.

Language allows you to adopt diverse perspectives on the many relationships that may exist between you as a subject and you as an object, using differing frames of perspective. These include "I am" and "you are," "here" and "there," "now" and "then." These perspectives give you a place to make sense of, and respond to, both internal needs or drives, and external events. This is crucial to your concept of who you are (McHugh, Stewart, and Almada 2019).

Now, as promised, you have been taken on a quick tour of language and its importance to perspective taking and your sense of self. It might be worth rereading a few times. Next, I invite you to go through a series of exercises to practice different aspects of perspective taking to reinforce these skills.

# Taking a More Flexible Perspective

This chapter asks a lot of you. Practices like these are important for learning these skills. They empower you to take on the next levels of challenge, as you free yourself from unnecessary burdens on your journey of self-forgiveness.

To find the most useful and powerful conception of who you are, you have a very adaptable mechanism to hold or make space for a story. At the same time, you can play with that story through a variety of perspectives. The following exercises will (1) build your skills in perspective taking, (2) draw on your three aspects of self, and (3) practice perspective taking that works.

Let's look at common perspectives that tend to trap us. For each perspective, I will share an example drawn from daily life. Consider the effects of the example, and then observe how you might be experiencing it. As you explore, identify which perspectives keep you hooked, and then consider how to use your skills to get unhooked

## *Perspective 1: This is just like that.*

"When I fail at my job, I feel like I am a complete fraud."

In this story, failing at your job is like declaring yourself to be a criminal (This *failure* is just like that *fraud*).

Do you think this is a useful perspective? Why might this perspective not help you work things out? Hint: Think of what you have been asked to practice regarding guilt.

______________________________________________

______________________________________________

______________________________________________

______________________________________________

______________________________________________

______________________________________________

Is this example of perspective taking more useful? "When I fail at my job, I feel like I am unskilled." While this is still a tough point of view, how might this perspective (*failure* equals *unskilled*) prompt a more useful response?

______________________________________________

______________________________________________

______________________________________________

______________________________________________

Do you have any *this is just like that* stories that get you stuck?

______________________________________________

______________________________________________

______________________________________________

______________________________________________

Write down another perspective that can help you rewrite those stories.

______

______

______

______

______

______

## *Perspective 2: This is different from that.*

"I am not like my friends; I am an impostor. I feel I am a total fake while my friends are all so authentic."

In this story, the impostor me is different from my authentic friends. What might be the outcome of this sort of perspective? Hint: Think about your work on shame.

______

______

______

______

______

The "I" in the story is comparing what I feel *internally* with what I see *externally* in my friends. These are different experiences. Try to accept discomfort about feeling fake. Also consider that your internal feelings and your external appearances are not always the same. As a result, others might also feel different internally from how they appear externally.

What might this perspective of *this is different from that* now produce? Consider this perspective and write down your response.

How does the *impostor/I am fake* story change?

Write down any *this is different from that* stories that get you stuck.

## *Perspective 3: This is opposite to that.*

Think of a monster story you might tell yourself, or a monster story you have seen in someone close to you—just pretend it is yours. Write it down briefly.

______________________________________________

______________________________________________

______________________________________________

______________________________________________

If this monster story tells you something true about you that you do not like, what would your opposite story point toward, if it were true? Would it point toward being or doing something you value? What would that opposite story be?

______________________________________________

______________________________________________

______________________________________________

______________________________________________

______________________________________________

## *Perspective 4: This is comparable to that (including same/different).*

Compare how you saw yourself influenced by your monster story with how a trusted friend may have seen you.

If you consider how your trusted friends actually treat you, how do these experiences compare with the thoughts, feelings, and sensations of being influenced by your monster story?

When you are doing something that authentically represents who you are at your best, how does that compare to the story of being influenced by your monster story?

## *Perspective 5: This builds on, or contributes to, that.*

Your distress regarding the monster story has likely stopped you from contributing to something that matters to you. If you were free from that story, what could you do?

_______________________________________________

_______________________________________________

_______________________________________________

_______________________________________________

_______________________________________________

What might the monster story you tell yourself protect you from (disappointment, failure, appearing vulnerable)? How does this keep you stuck?

_______________________________________________

_______________________________________________

_______________________________________________

_______________________________________________

If your distress regarding the monster story could be transformed to help you act in an authentic way to serve something greater, what experience of value could that build?

_______________________________________________

_______________________________________________

_______________________________________________

_______________________________________________

## *Perspective 6: I can look at this from a different point in time, whether before/after, now/then, present/past, present/future, future/past.*

If you have failed at one point, and later had success in that same area, what would that future successful you say to that past you who failed? Write about that experience.

______________________________________________

______________________________________________

______________________________________________

______________________________________________

______________________________________________

______________________________________________

How would your past self have reacted to hearing that?

______________________________________________

______________________________________________

______________________________________________

If you could look at what you are going through now from a perspective of you ten years ago or ten years into the future, what would that past or future you think of what you are experiencing right now?

______________________________________________

______________________________________________

______________________________________________

______________________________________________

If you were at the end of your life, say at age ninety-five, what would your perspective be about your monster story of today?

## *Perspective 7: I can look at this from a different point in space, as where I am physically affects my perspective.*

If you are really stuck in a place because of any one of the stories you have told so far, imagine if you stood outside yourself, as a bystander to your experience. How would that change things? What would your experience look like if you saw it from a distance?

If your view of yourself was obstructed and you could not see everything, where would you need to stand to get the whole story?

Is there a particular place that evokes a story for you (a school, hospital, city, street)? Is there a particular place that allows you to feel authentic (a forest, a friend's house, a sacred space)? Write about meaningful places that evoke stories or experiences.

## *Perspective 8: Self and Other (I am/Here/Now) and (You/There/Then)*

Focus on your breathing to bring your attention to where you are, here in space at this time. What is it like to experience being in this present moment: *I am/Here/Now*?

To what extent are you actually present with your experience of *I am/Here/Now* at any given moment?

If a particular story from the past captures you, what is it like to experience being in that moment: *You/There/Then*? How does that experience stop you from being fully present: *I am/ Here/Now*?

---

---

---

## *Perspective 9: Does this cause that? Does this set the conditions for that?*

Think about the monster story you have told. What might precede your experience of the monster story? For example, *I walked through the door and saw what a good time my friends were having, and I thought,* I don't belong there because I am…

---

---

---

Recall that preceding monster story (or thought, sensation, emotion, image). Now instead of treating the monster story as your reality, what would it be like to respond as your authentic self? Take a few moments to imagine that, then write about it.

---

---

---

---

---

---

Each of these exercises in perspective taking can be useful in opening up more options to respond to life circumstances, whether those of the past, of the present, or emerging in the future. The next series of exercises will prompt you to consider how you might freely apply them to life events in order to forgive yourself.

## Perspectives in the Labyrinth of Your Life

We have discussed monsters in dark places. In one of the great myths, Minotaur was a bull-headed, half-man, half-beast—a product of the union between an immortal and a mortal. Minotaur was a much-feared guardian of a treasure held within the maze of a dark underground labyrinth. Walking this labyrinth is a metaphor for the process of journeying within, and the monsters we must face, to transform our lives and reach the treasure—who we truly are. Let's begin by considering Lani's story.

> *Lani wanted to face what was hidden in her history. As one of millions of families displaced by the wars and revolutions of the twentieth century, her family bore deep scars. As the English-speaking child of refugee parents, she was responsible for interpreting for her parents, even negotiating their various legal and tax obligations. She felt torn by the obligations of her originating culture on one hand, and by the freedoms of the new world in which they lived on the other. Lani simultaneously needed to care for her children and extended family, yet also had a desire to pursue her love of traveling to ancient sites in the world, to study them. This felt important to her, regardless of her family's opinions or needs. At the core of this conundrum was the labyrinth she must at last walk through.*

In the chart that follows, Lani describes her stories, identifies their perspective, and begins opening to alternate stories. The exercise brings her closer to the treasure in the labyrinth: knowing who she truly is.

| Story | Perspective | Alternate Story |
|---|---|---|
| *I am stuck within family and culture.* | *This builds on or contributes to that.* | *My culture informs who I am but does not control who I am. It gives me a base from which I can explore.* |
| *My parents' work took away the love I needed.* | *This is just like that.* | *Hard work does not mean there is no love. When I work hard, I can also make deliberate time to love my children. I know I am worthy of loving and being loved.* |
| *When I see my friends, I feel I made stupid choices.* | *This is comparable to that (includes same/different).* | *When I put myself in the shoes of my friends and see how they compare themselves to me, they see someone who took risks, tried different things, and has two beautiful children.* |
| *I am making all the sacrifices to keep the family afloat.* | *Does this cause that?* | *Being responsible does not make me feel bad. Being with someone who does not take responsibility? That is the thing I need to work on.* |
| *The call to care for war victims wracks my conscience.* | *I look at this from a different point in space.* | *I know the helplessness of distance and isolation. From this safe place, I feel deeply how insecure people are in war zones. I will continue my work to help them in a practical way.* |

Like Lani, you can use this chart to take perspective and write an alternate story. At http://www.newharbinger.com/45694, you will find a blank version of this chart to download and complete as many times as you like. Try coming closer to your own self by exploring your alternate story.

| Story | Perspective | Alternate Story |
|---|---|---|
| | | |
| | | |
| | | |
| | | |
| | | |

Prepare yourself for this experience of facing your monster by bringing attention to your breath. As you inhale and exhale through your nose, breathe compassion and loving-kindness into every part of your being, both body and mind.

Once you have completed the chart, choose an experience from it that is moderately challenging. Allow a range of inner experiences about what is challenging in that situation to flow through your consciousness. If at any point, this exercise becomes overwhelming, bring yourself to a safe place where you are able to respond to your experience in a way that enables you to function well. If you are feeling safe, meditate on observing your thoughts, images, emotions, and bodily sensations without getting bound up in them.

Follow these prompts as you continue to observe your internal experience. Maintaining your mindful state, write down what you are noticing and the names you give the experiences.

Name the story that is involved in those experiences.

________________________________________

________________________________________

________________________________________

________________________________________

________________________________________

Name the images that arise, perhaps from memory or fears of the future.

________________________________________

________________________________________

________________________________________

________________________________________

Name the emotions that arise, as they arise.

______________________________________________

______________________________________________

______________________________________________

______________________________________________

Name the bodily sensations you feel.

______________________________________________

______________________________________________

______________________________________________

______________________________________________

Notice that you are having an experience. What is it like?

______________________________________________

______________________________________________

______________________________________________

______________________________________________

______________________________________________

Observe that you are noticing the you that is having the experience. What do you understand about this viewpoint?

______________________________________________

______________________________________________

______________________________________________

______________________________________________

Now take a different perspective on those experiences. To the person having those experiences, you can be a friend, you can be the future you or the past you, you can be a wise person or a mentor. Choose any perspective that allows you to see these experiences from a different point of view. Without being harsh, critical, or judgmental, describe the experience you have of taking another perspective.

________________________________________

________________________________________

________________________________________

________________________________________

________________________________________

________________________________________

________________________________________

________________________________________

Meditate on those stories using the processes you have been practicing. If your attention drifts, bring it gently back to the story.

As you will see, if you keep practicing these skills, each perspective reveals a new treasure. *The Alchemist*, a story of transformation through adventure, reveals that new perspectives on old things can reveal many treasures, especially knowledge, self-belief, and unfolding destiny (Coelho 1988). Through this revelation, you gain meaning and application of your life purpose.

# An Expanded Sense of Self

So far, you have been undertaking a journey within by learning about the power of story, the way to see it with compassion, and now how to expand your sense of self. This expanded set of skills and sense of self allows you to develop perspectives that help you examine how things fit together in a way that works, take into account all the things contributing to an event or experience, and increase your flexibility to respond to what life brings next.

This is the great work of alchemy that you are exploring—the gift of transforming an experience that may have been dark, useless, discarded, rejected, or unhealthy into something that is worthy of consideration and care. In the course of this workbook, you have already been revealing what you value in yourself and in your life experience. In the next chapter, you will work further on these revelations. Self-forgiveness becomes an ongoing theme for your life as you become able to clearly identify your values, flexibly apply them to a life that is responsive to your needs, and meet the demands placed upon you by the world's continual challenges.

CHAPTER 4

# Understand What You Truly Value

Our values can be guiding lights we use to navigate life choices. If a ship's captain ignores a lighthouse signal, the ship may veer toward the rocks. Similarly, when our values are ignored, undermined, or transgressed against, toxic self-blame can flourish, taking us toward the metaphorical rocks.

If others have been hurt by your actions, you may not have acted in accord with your values about relationships and caring for others. Even deeper, you may hold values for yourself that you have not followed in your own life and decision-making. In this chapter, you will be given the opportunity to explore your values, learn from hard-won experiences, and develop your insight as you continue this journey. Understanding what you truly value gives you effective leverage to make the life changes you need to make. Clarity about your values allows you to take steps toward your liberation.

You have been working with storytelling, compassion, and perspective, which are all skills that can be used at any time to build your insight and understanding of what you value. To free yourself from toxic self-blame, you have been forming a basis for genuine acceptance. Being accepted just as you are is a gateway to a sense of liberation. When you direct this respect, acceptance, and empathy toward yourself, it helps you do the work needed to drop unnecessary burdens. Then, clarifying what you value ensures that your self-forgiveness is liberating from a deep place of your truth. This liberation helps inform you so you can make the decisions you need to live out your life's meaning and purpose.

## Reflecting on a Meaningful Life

You have distinctive views of life, and talents and abilities to offer. As a result, you pursue a unique life. It is yours to live out as you understand it. An age-old question that you may have considered is: what is the meaning of life? This question can be helpful, as to know the meaning of life is to understand the unique contribution you have to make to the world and the experience of meaning as you know it. A sense of purpose arises from engaging in making that contribution, within your context and your community, to the extent you can. Take some time to reflect on this view on meaning and purpose, and write out your reflections on this challenge. Examples include:

- Charlize values breaking the cycle of addiction and violence and building a family of her own with a supportive partner, a family in which she can make a contribution in her career focused on meeting her clients' needs.
- Lisette values supporting others as a counselor and wishes to offer her clients skills that enable them to fulfill their life's calling.
- Derrick wants to live purposefully, especially living life according to his values in his relationship, where he wants to live with vulnerability, strength, and open communication.

What is the meaning of life to you?

______________________________________________________________________

______________________________________________________________________

______________________________________________________________________

______________________________________________________________________

______________________________________________________________________

______________________________________________________________________

______________________________________________________________________

______________________________________________________________________

You will return to this reflection frequently in your life. A practice of reflecting on a meaningful life is helpful at the open and close of each day. The reflection can also happen over much longer time frames, as years or decades pass. Consider what might be a useful time and place for you to reflect on your life. There is great benefit on the self-forgiveness journey if you consciously reflect as you engage in the various cycles of life that are important to you, whether daily, weekly, monthly, key life projects, life events, life relationships—whatever is useful to you.

# Moving Toward Values-Based Action

Victor Frankl had developed his theories in his ordinary prewar life. However, the war gave him the powerful proof he needed that the search for meaning and purpose is a key driver of a fulfilling life, in both ordinary and extraordinary circumstances. Despite losing every possession, many people he loved, and control of his life's direction, he still had "the last of the human freedoms—to choose one's attitude in any given set of circumstances, to choose one's own way." Frankl built on this experience of being able to take perspective. It is an example of a values-based response to his meaning and purpose. The values he chose to direct his life were growth and freedom.

Frankl repeatedly witnessed people who engaged in everyday acts of heroism based on their values. He saw people give their last morsel of bread to another or comfort the dying despite being within an inch of death themselves (Frankl 1985). These actions demonstrate values that inform both outward behavior and inward care. These acts of heroism were gateways to life-giving opportunities for those who made those values-based responses to others. In turn, the acts allowed them freedom to maintain their humanity and grow as people despite the horror of their experiences.

Your core values are the ways of being in the world that are ultimately most important to you, and they shape attitudes that inform your behavior and action. Attitudes, behaviors, actions, and values can be mutually reinforcing. Values that inform a rich and fulfilling life are those ways of being that you know are true to your innermost core, to your heart. These might be drives for health, justice, learning, relationships, contribution, and care, among many other priorities.

Your values are yours and do not need to be justified to others. Holding a value is like having a favorite food or color, a preference for a type of pet, the sort of things you like to do to relax. Ultimately you will know what is true for you and what choices you want to make (Harris 2006).

Values are not goals. Values have a quality of always being brought into being. Goals are something we attain. Building a house is a goal to be achieved. Once the house is built, the goal disappears. Wanting to make a home for your family is an ongoing process, a value that remains. It may be refined as the family grows and changes. Values inform how you live your life, both in the moment and on an ongoing basis. They are like a compass that allows you to navigate when you are both on and off course in your life. For example, the value of being a good friend requires a variety of attitudes and behaviors, like being open, being a good listener, being trustworthy and trusting, to name a few of the limitless qualities of friendship. Each of these inform you and is like a compass that can tell you if you are moving in the right direction with your friendship. And when you get off track, values reveal which way to turn to get back on track.

To start to explore this, take some time to write about three values you believe you hold. As you do, consider what is most important about how you treat yourself or others.

Value 1 ____________________________________________

____________________________________________

Value 2 ____________________________________________

____________________________________________

Value 3 ____________________________________________

____________________________________________

## Understanding Your Values

The skills of reviewing your story, using a compassionate lens, and perspective taking help you understand the power of language to build your system of values in response to your needs and the world around you (Hayes 2019). You will learn rules from family, culture, and life experience that help inform your values, which in turn inform your actions. Sometimes these rules form instantaneously; for example, *Don't touch things that have been heating on a stove*, and sometimes over a long period, such as, *What I give to others comes back in spades.* This chapter will give you building blocks to understand what you have learned about values, and to consider what new things you may wish to learn.

*Lani found that she held certain values about money management, wealth creation, and relationships. She thought making money and building family were exclusive of each other, that money got in the way of relationships. These values were protecting her from hurt and loss. But by giving her story respect, a compassionate lens, and a new perspective, she saw that she needed to master both personal and business finances to protect her children and build a home where she could raise them with love and attention.*

*After undertaking this shift, Lani found a high-paying position at a research facility looking at how to support displaced people. She was able to talk to, influence, and raise funds for transformative and practical programs that assisted thousands. This transformation led to an enrichment in how she viewed herself, how managing money could be beneficial, and how she could more flexibly respond to life's demands. Lani now knew that she could refine her values as she developed financial competence, learned more about business, and created a supportive space in which she could follow her professional pathway and also express her love for her family.*

Values are adaptive. When you experience your values, like Lani did, they give you a direction for action and a reason to take action. The active nature of a compass guides your pursuit of the things you yearn for and desire. At its best, acting in line with your values forms a self-reinforcing cycle of motivation and fulfillment (McHugh, Stewart, and Almada 2019). When you freely consider your values, allowing them to inform your direction and choices, you form a basis for the flexibility you need to respond to life challenges. You free up your ability to allocate effort to what is truly important to you.

Considering your values gives you a perspective on how you learn, create new rules, and guide your behavior. Reflecting on your values helps you take action that works in response to opportunities you want to pursue and pitfalls you wish to avoid (Barnes-Holmes, Hayes, and Dymond 2001). When usefully directed in this way, values are the foundation for responding to toxic self-blame. As you move through life, the sense of direction builds pathways that prevent relapse, through making values-based choices for acting and achieving goals that are true to who you are (Woodyatt and Wenzel 2014).

To emphasize the difference between goals that can be fulfilled and values that give direction, consider this example. Say you want to find a friend—that is a goal to be achieved. Values have a quality of something you wish to move toward but may never fully obtain. If you seek vulnerability in a friendship, that is a value (Harris 2011). Life always brings hurdles to test how you show up in a variety of challenging circumstances. You may want to be able to be completely vulnerable with a trusted friend. However, if you are unsure of the motives of your new friend, vulnerability may be something you need to moderate. Let's consider how Lani's values helped her navigate a challenge.

*In her new job, Lani had to travel to remote, isolated locations. She had to drive all-terrain vehicles as a safety measure. She also needed to work on her strength and fitness since the travel could be arduous. The long driver training, boot camps, and distance running took her away from her children. While the separation was a cause for concern, she balanced her competing values and had a deep talk with her children about what she was doing and why. They talked about the unbreakable bond of love they shared wherever they all were, and decided together to start a family blog. They posted Lani's adventures to their many cousins, aunts, and uncles, talking about her adventures, her important work, and how proud they were of their mother. Her work, instead of taking her away from her children, brought them closer together. Flexibly managing her seemingly conflicted values built new possibility.*

Life will test your values, both when you apply them or fail to apply them. For example, when you have a value of self-protection or being true to yourself, when you refuse to do something you do not agree with, there may be consequences or backlash—internal or external. Think back to Lisette, who was again pressured to host her family for a celebration. Yet, without family recognition or response to her needs for respect and inclusion, she knew she had to honor her values about self-care and say no. In this case, Lisette's values about caring for others needed to be balanced with her developing values of self-care. And she needed to stand by her decision, even when her mother and sisters started calling her, continually insisting about her contributing to family events.

Your values-based approach to difficult situations affords you a place of reflection, even if that action was or will be difficult. However, if you go along with the crowd and ignore what is true for you, that too will highlight your values. When you experience remorse or regret for an action not in line with your values, begin asking what value is voicing itself. The following examples show that life, as a process, is continually teaching you and testing your values.

Values include your soul's yearnings and heart's desires. Yearnings and desires are drivers for action, shaping how you wish to be and act within your life (Hayes 2019).

*Charlize longed to feel both safe within her family and secure in her health. She was so fearful of the history of addiction in her family that she made a rule that family gatherings at her house would be both sober and alcohol free. When her brother arrived affected by alcohol, she did not allow him inside. She sent a strong message that day. And most of her family respected it.*

Values inform how you wish to treat yourself, to be treated, and how you wish to treat others.

*In his relationship, Derrick longed to be treated with respect and to have a bond that can be trusted. However, he had found that when he and his partner did not agree, they ignored each other or had petty arguments. She would not attend either counseling or classes about communication and relationship building. Derrick had to make a choice based on his values. He wanted a relationship where he and his partner were willing to cooperate, share, and grow, so he sought individual counseling and began exploring how he might begin the process of separation.*

Each of these examples shows that values encompass qualities you wish to develop and perfect. In turn, values inform, guide, and bring into being that which you yearn for. This yearning informs what you believe to be most important in your life and the way in which you wish to face life and its challenges and circumstances (Hayes 2019).

The qualities of values that we have discussed are one of the key leverage points for both toxic self-blame and liberating self-forgiveness. Values are on display to others through the way you respond to life circumstances, and they are also deeply held where no one can see but you. While values can inspire, guide, and motivate you, failures to put your values into action can condemn, block, and demoralize you. Your values can propel you to life experiences that are fulfilling, but they can also confront you with experiences of darkness and loss.

*Charlize was driven by her values to be healthy and clear minded, and as a result she developed a strict rule that meant excluding all opiate use, even if it was short-term for postoperative pain relief. One value—being clean and sober—undermined her recovery from injury. Examining her story, putting on a compassionate lens, and taking different perspectives allowed Charlize to have a broader view and lighten the burden she was bearing.*

In this way, even if you are contemplating how you might have transgressed against your values, there is still a signpost for an alternate pathway, something restorative for your "transgression," or moving in a different direction toward the valued action that is your heart's desire. This process is at the core of how you wrestle with your experiences and internal conflicts. For example, that which disgusts you (for Charlize, her disgust with the effects of excessive alcohol) indicates what you might need to move away from, or may indicate what you need to move toward in a way that is healthy and beneficial for you.

Consider something that is unpleasant for you and write it down.

________________________________________

Identify its opposite or an alternate and describe it.

________________________________________.

Does this contrast provide insight into what you do value? Reflect on what this repulsion reveals.

________________________________________

________________________________________

________________________________________

________________________________________

________________________________________

________________________________________

________________________________________

________________________________________

________________________________________

________________________________________

This exercise applies the perspective-taking practice: *This is not like that.* The practice of perspective-taking skills will continue to help you grow in your ability to make values-based choices that build the life you want.

# What Actions Not in Accord with Your Values Can Reveal

Your life journey will bring you into contact with your values, sometimes on a moment-to-moment basis. Some small examples: What time did you set the alarm for? Do you snooze the alarm? Do you go back to sleep? Do you exercise first thing? Shower? Cook breakfast? Stick to routine? Each of these small decisions might connect you to your system of values about self-care, nutrition, work ethic, and so on. This experience is useful most of the time. However, when you hold values closely but are not acting in accordance with them, your experience can be uncomfortable.

If you are not doing things that accord with your values, you can be challenged with the experience of being an impostor. Typically, impostors say or believe they are one thing but act in another way, perhaps in a way that is deceptive and misleading. However, if you tell yourself that you are an impostor, the great irony is that once you examine the story, it often contains the key elements you need to discover the pathways to your true calling. One of the signposts for your journey of self-forgiveness is the discovery of your deeply held values, perhaps in the beliefs you have, the way you act, or the intentions you are trying to fulfill. For example, when Malcolm was feeling deeply guilty, thinking about how he had let his father down, he felt like an impostor at being a father to his own children. When he examined this story with a compassionate lens, he found this story indicated his value about being supportive to those he loves.

When you are discovering your values as guiding elements to your inner life, pain confirms that you are not aligned with your "truth." This allows you to live with yourself in good conscience, which is a great, liberating experience (Hayes 2019).

Let's start the process of clarifying what some of your primary values might be. This is not an exhaustive process, as life has a way of challenging you in unexpected ways that reveal values in unique circumstances. The following list is a brief indicator of values identified by Dr. Russ Harris (2011). Some may be true for you, some may be irrelevant, some may unfold as life happens. As you read this list, circle the values that inspire and motivate you. Do any feel like a compass you guide your life by?

**Acceptance:** to be open to and accepting of myself, others, life

**Assertiveness:** to respectfully stand up for my rights and request what I want

**Authenticity:** to be authentic, genuine, real; to be true to myself

**Beauty:** to appreciate, create, nurture, or cultivate beauty in myself, others, the environment

**Caring:** to be caring toward myself, others, the environment

**Compassion:** to act with kindness toward those who are suffering

**Courage:** to be courageous or brave; to persist in the face of fear, threat, or difficulty

**Curiosity:** to be curious, open-minded, and interested; to explore and discover

**Encouragement:** to encourage and reward behavior that I value in myself or others

**Forgiveness:** to be forgiving toward myself or others

**Freedom:** to live freely; to choose how I live and behave, or help others do likewise

**Friendliness:** to be friendly, companionable, or agreeable toward others

**Fun:** to be fun-loving; to seek, create, and engage in fun-filled activities

**Generosity:** to be generous, sharing, and giving to myself or others

**Honesty:** to be honest, truthful, and sincere with myself and others

**Humility:** to be humble or modest; to let my achievements speak for themselves

**Humor:** to see and appreciate the humorous side of life

**Intimacy:** to open up, reveal, and share myself—emotionally or physically—in my close personal relationships

**Justice:** to uphold justice and fairness

**Kindness:** to be kind, compassionate, considerate, nurturing or caring toward myself or others

**Love:** to act lovingly or affectionately toward myself or others

**Mindfulness:** to be conscious of, open to, and curious about my here-and-now experience

**Order:** to be orderly and organized

**Patience:** to wait calmly for what I want

**Reciprocity:** to build relationships in which there is a fair balance of giving and taking

**Respect:** to be respectful toward myself or others; to be polite, considerate, and show positive regard

**Self-awareness:** to be aware of my own thoughts, feelings, and actions

**Skillfulness:** to continually practice and improve my skills, and apply myself fully when using them

**Spirituality:** to connect with things bigger than myself

**Trust:** to be trustworthy; to be loyal, faithful, sincere, and reliable

Select two or three primary values that have a deep meaning to you. Write them here.

________________________________________

________________________________________

Describe an area of your life where you might refine or better define and express those values.

________________________________________

________________________________________

________________________________________

________________________________________

Choose one or two values that are important for you to work on.

______________________________________________

______________________________________________

Now revisit your story. Is there a way your values are challenging you?

______________________________________________

______________________________________________

______________________________________________

Might this value be prompting you to do something in your life? Write down some ideas.

______________________________________________

______________________________________________

______________________________________________

What one or two actions might you take that will make these values come to life?

______________________________________________

______________________________________________

Now, if you are ready, return to a place of discomfort. This is the place of toxic self-blame or the wider stories that perhaps include the feeling of being an impostor. It's where Malcolm guiltily reflected on parenting. Whatever discomfort you are experiencing brought you to this journey of self-forgiveness, where there are a wealth of discoveries to be found. By getting in touch with the darkness, and bringing light to your experience, you are developing skills in understanding your values. Even when you intensely dislike what you are going through, that dislike points to a value you hold. If you do not like being disrespected, respect is a possible value for you. If you do not like someone ignoring your opinion, being heard might be another value. And if you do not like your own behavior, such as being caught up in gossip, then maybe you have a value about integrity, privacy, or openness.

Whatever the darkness of your experience, when you bring a sense of lightness, openness, and curiosity to what you are experiencing, at some point you will uncover the values you hold. In each of the following examples of discomfort, there is a possible value to be discovered.

| Discomfort | Emotion | Values-Based Need |
|---|---|---|
| *I have done something wrong, and I have not set it right.* | *Remorse* | *I am responsible in my life, and this wrong is an area I can work on.* |
| *I do not like an action/ circumstance/experience.* | *Regret* | *I am curious about my regret, and I want to learn from this experience and respond effectively.* |
| *I shift responsibility for this mistake to my "self."* | *Self-blame* | *I want to understand what contributed to this mistake, allocate appropriate responsibility, and take action.* |
| *I have broken something.* | *Guilt* | *I have a value of restoration and want to make it right.* |
| *I am broken.* | *Shame* | *I have a value of self-care and want to heal and restore myself.* |
| *I intensely dislike or hate myself.* | *Self-loathing* | *I have a value of developing and applying self-acceptance and self-compassion to this place of distress.* |
| *I find myself revolting and repulsive.* | *Self-disgust* | *I have a value of being understanding toward myself so I can find a way to heal what sickens me.* |

Do you have an area of secret discomfort that makes you feel like an impostor? The values you discover are the compass to guide you out of the swamp of unforgiveness, toward yourself. Write down your story of discomfort.

______________________________________________

______________________________________________

______________________________________________

______________________________________________

What are your values to be discovered in your story? You can use this chart or download a blank copy at http://www.newharbinger.com/45694.

| Discomfort | Emotion | Values-Based Need |
|---|---|---|
| | | |
| | | |
| | | |
| | | |
| | | |
| | | |
| | | |

What might this impostor story tell you about the pathways you need to take to refine, clarify, and strengthen your values?

______________________________________________

______________________________________________

______________________________________________

What actions can you take to start building this alternate life pathway?

______________________________________________

______________________________________________

______________________________________________

As you explore, you may find that values are not a neutral experience. Values have the nature of being fragments of an active conscience that may speak to you in many ways. You have been able to contemplate that values can provide signposts to both liberation and isolation, depending on how you are responding to life and what values you hold. An important skill that is underpinned by the use of a compassionate lens is to allow yourself to experience your distress and not get caught up in it as you engage in perspective taking. Exploring this experience of distress with compassion and acceptance provides for an alternative point of view, which helps in the process of discovering, comparing, and prioritizing values that give you a pathway forward (Villatte, Villatte, and Hayes 2016). For example, when Gerard was in a bicycle accident, he discovered that one of his values was caring for his family and not wanting to be a burden. At first, his dependence on others was an emotionally painful experience, and not helpful for his healing. He needed to balance this value with self-care and perspective gained from valuing his survival.

In both life-giving and painful experiences, you have been able to consider how values help you begin the process of carefully examining what brings you a fulfilling life. Where you find yourself acting in alignment with your values, this may bring you to a place of new discovery and expansion.

Describe a time, now or in the past, when you actively implemented your values in a venture that was life giving to you.

---

---

---

How did this alignment give you a sense of discovery or expansion, or another way of informing your life direction?

---

---

---

There can also be the need to reflect on the priority you give values. Sometimes the big challenge is not doing the wrong thing, it is choosing between two things that are right. For example, you may excessively pursue a performance goal in your sport, prioritizing that goal over the need for your body to recover. Or you may take care of another, but not take care of yourself.

From your list of values, choose an area that needs more prioritization. Write it here.

---

Do you have a value that somehow undermines something else that is needed in your life? For example, if you say, "I like feeling safe," but you also do not want to live a small life, then there is an implied value that you want to live a life that is adventurous and expansive. Write down the two conflicting values.

1. ______________________________

2. ______________________________

When you are confronted by values that are seemingly in conflict, what might you be trading off for not pursuing a valued, but challenging, life pathway?

______________________________________________________________________

______________________________________________________________________

______________________________________________________________________

______________________________________________________________________

## When You Don't Feel Safe Within Yourself

A common response to the failure to act in accordance with your values is a sense of shame. Shame may be held publicly or secretly. It is a key outcome of the impostor story, as it is closely linked to your sense of self and your moral responsibilities. Unfortunately, the experience of having human consciousness also gives you the experience of automatic and unbidden discomfort that arises from thoughts, images, emotions, and bodily sensations.

You learn throughout life that there are many threats that can harm you. Modern technology brings those threats into your most personal places through images and interactions facilitated by that same technology. Your power to make connections through perspective taking can also make you feel unsafe within yourself. An example of this is when you automatically link things—*this is like that*, a noise outside is like an intruder trying to break in—but it is just the cat knocking over a flowerpot.

This becomes a problem if you are constantly making those links. You will create a space where you not only feel unsafe in that space, you may not feel safe within yourself. A core value of living beings is a sense of safety within self. So having a mind filled with thoughts that you do not like how you think, feel, or perceive is a place for an internal fracture with your sense of values.

This workbook uses the exploration of your values as a place for restoration. You are perfect as you are, with all your qualities, including your imperfections and limitations. Processes of self-acceptance, supported by self-compassion, give you the freedom you need to reframe this automatic experience of internal and external perspective taking and perception of your life challenges (Bennett 2015).

Values can be violated either through action or inaction. Failure to act according to your values can undermine your sense of being true to who you are (Hayes 2019). To restate: what you need to forgive yourself for may not have involved anyone else, but rather you have hurt yourself by an action or inaction that goes against your values. You have been practicing skills to reframe these events through perspective taking informed by your values. This does not ignore others, your family, your context, your community, as you will have a wide range of values that help you live life in its fullest sense, and may in turn be a focus of your development and expansion. So let's create alternate stories about fears that reflect your values and your preferred life outcomes.

Look at what your fear is protecting and envision what that might look like if there was success. If, for example, you fear failure, you might envision one more of these alternatives:

- Failures teach me lessons about my values.
- I can learn from setbacks.
- Understanding my values can help me get around barriers.
- When I fail, I reach my goals through doing what I value.
- Even if I fail, I am succeeding when I do what I value because then I can learn.

Now reflect on one of your stories that may need an alternate.

Fear story: ______________________________________________

______________________________________________

______________________________________________

Alternate success stories: ______________________________________________

______________________________________________

______________________________________________

This exercise uses the skills you have practiced to take action based on your values. You are learning to respond to an experience that can be quite unpleasant: fear. Within that fear is a lesson to be learned.

## Rebuilding Self-Trust

The key to opening the door of genuine self-forgiveness requires you to rebuild the experience of self-trust, which is at the heart of reconciling all the different parts of you into a whole being that is centered and congruent with your core values. Undertaking values-based reconciliation within your self is the engine that begins the work of clearing away toxic self-blame. It aligns your sense of self at all levels: your expansive self, your story self, and your functional self. The work of reconciliation is driven by new perspectives on the big challenges, struggles, and painful events of your life. It puts in place values-based changes that are the beginning of work on genuine self-forgiveness (Wenzel, Woodyatt, and Hedrick 2012).

This process is adaptive, as your choice to develop your own approach to a life based on attitudes informed by your values will give life to yourself and others. A response to life that is based deeply in openheartedness and the vulnerability of your values will allow you to explore choice with freedom. These choices reflect the core values that will build life-giving experiences.

The next chapter will help you further refine your skills. You will practice some evidence-based, actionable ways to get unstuck and drop unnecessary burdens. Along the way, you will develop the willingness to take on difficult but necessary tasks, as you learn to bring your attention to the present moment while also expanding and making room for the challenges life sends your way. Going forward, your efforts will draw on your values as you take action to build a life that works for you, not against you.

CHAPTER 5

# Free Yourself from Responses That Poison You

You have been on a journey of discovery in order to free yourself from experiences and burdens that are toxic. With the skills you honed in previous chapters, you now have resources to expand your ability to respond to toxicity, such as self-blame, guilt, self-criticism, and condemning yourself. With some simple, effective approaches, you can become free from what is poisoning your life. As you will discover, what may have been toxic can be turned into a treasure that helps you build the life you want.

Consider some of your responses to painful events and feelings that are toxic or poisonous to you. Recall the way Lani responded to the challenges of work and money in a way that brought her down. Charlize was crippled by doubts about health and addiction. Derrick was captured by loyalty to his family over his own needs. Lisette was caught up in her story of not being good enough. Malcolm was stuck in deep shame and guilt about his father's suicide.

Go ahead and describe three key ways you have responded to pain that continue to poison you and hold you back.

Response 1: ______________________________________________

______________________________________________

______________________________________________

Response 2: ______________________________________________

______________________________________________

______________________________________________

Response 3: ______________________________________________

______________________________________________

______________________________________________

Now consider your responses. Identify the value you have that is being closed down by responses that are poisoning you. For example, Charlize's fear of addiction took over her values about healing and recovery. Derrick's need to be loyal to his family overshadowed his values of transparency and caring attention in his intimate relationship. Lisette's service to her family impacted her value of caring for her own needs. Lani was so transfixed by her vision of a perfect family that she abandoned her values of personal development and growth.

The value I'm closing down with my first response is: ___________________________

The value I'm closing down with my second response is: ___________________________

The value I'm closing down with my third response is: ___________________________

Notice whether there are common threads in the responses that are undermining your values. Name any common threads you want to work on.

___________________________________________________________________________

___________________________________________________________________________

___________________________________________________________________________

___________________________________________________________________________

___________________________________________________________________________

___________________________________________________________________________

You have shown courage in meeting the challenge of each of these exercises. Now you will use this information to practice new skills. For each, you will be asked to put into practice what you have already learned. To help you expand your insights and respond in new ways, you can use the examples as guides for reflecting on your own journey. Keep a compassionate lens as you go: be kind to yourself as if talking to someone you love—a good friend, family member, or your children. Doing this will help reveal the actions you wish to take.

Similarly, the skills of perspective taking will support confronting, befriending, and even embracing your internal monsters (Harris 2006). This embrace informs the values-based action you will use to build your future. Each time you begin a new action, your ability to take perspective will repeatedly bring fresh insights into undiscovered facets of your old stories. These insights about your values help you learn new ways to respond to past challenges. Where you have been held back and felt diminished, you will be able to expand and transform your story.

Let's begin exploring acceptance and the willingness to take on difficult but necessary tasks. Dropping unhelpful approaches and burdens requires that you develop your attention to the present moment, expand into willingness, and make room for the challenges life sends your way. You will do this while standing on the foundation of your values, so you take actions that work for you.

# Accept and Transform Your Experience

There is a paradox in psychology: people only become ready for change when they are genuinely accepted just as they are (Rogers 1942). On your journey of self-forgiveness, this paradox presents a major challenge because you have a well-practiced process of internal criticism. Now that you are in contact with the values you hold, in the presence of any pain and suffering you have experienced, you can respond to your story in a new way.

Self-acceptance has the quality of making a place for yourself, holding a space open, or even giving hospitality to someone. It is not about tolerating bad behavior or putting up with abuse. Instead, it is a respectful place for exploring your experience with openness, interest, and curiosity. Applying these qualities to your own journey takes away a layer of unnecessary distress; for example, being ashamed about being ashamed, being worried about being worried, or being depressed about being depressed. You can be willing to make space for your distress, whatever form it takes. As you have been practicing, you can be open, curious, and interested about the story that gives rise to this distress.

*Lisette was ashamed that she felt so bad about the holiday season and its challenges. She considered her values of caring for others and offering others a safe place for their distress. This led her to decide to extend this value to her own self-care. With this perspective, she could see that she would never encourage anyone else to tolerate the way her family treated her. Then she considered another value revealed by her anger: she needed to protect herself and set boundaries. Lisette felt both liberated and challenged by a new response. She had some work to do.*

Reflect on at least one of your painful stories. How might you have approached this distress differently?

___

___

___

___

What layer of distress (for example, anger, shame, worry, depression) can you remove through acceptance?

___

___

What are the values this distress reveals?

___

___

Does this awareness shift your experience of your story? Write about any new perspectives that result.

___

___

___

___

As you can see, there are many values involved in how we open up, or close down, to experience. In the presence of a distressing thought, feeling, experience, or bodily sensation, willingness can engage you in a process of opening up to a necessary challenge. This is how Charlize experienced it.

*As Charlize felt conflicted about her health, with her fear of addiction amidst the need for painkillers and surgical intervention, she realized these needs were both valid. They were based on a value of gaining and maintaining health. Charlize's challenge was to overcome the overwhelming anxiety and fear that had closed her down. This reaction arose from her experience of family distress, things she had witnessed, and taking responsibility for the actions of others. With willingness, she opened up to her primary need: to recover from her chronic condition. She researched and sought advice on pain relief, prescribed use, and close medical supervision. Once she was able to make a space for her valid feelings of fear and anxiety about addiction, she could at last commit to the surgery she needed.*

Consider a challenge you need to face. Are you willing to open up to a valued course of action? Choose an experience that may be closing you down, and reflect on how making space for it might change your perspective and experience.

______________________________

______________________________

______________________________

______________________________

______________________________

Identify a value that will enable you to take action on this challenge.

______________________________

______________________________

What action might you take to meet this challenge that reflects your values?

______________________________

______________________________

______________________________

Have you noticed any shift in your experience of your story as a result of exploring this challenge?

_______________________________________________

_______________________________________________

_______________________________________________

Well done! Through your acceptance and willingness, you can embrace your experience rather than having to change it or to judge it as either right or wrong. No matter what the experience is, there is something to learn from it. Everything you experience can teach you about what you value. Here's how Derrick learned this.

*Derrick was so caught in deep regrets about his relationship that when an old friend took him out for a meal, he couldn't enjoy it. After he talked nonstop about his troubles, his friend said, kindly but firmly, that Derrick was too lost in his regrets to even be in the present moment, sharing a nice dinner. Derrick realized that he had decided to take action and leave the relationship, but was sidetracked by his regretful thoughts. He asked this trusted friend to keep in touch as he initiated the breakup.*

*Through this process, Derrick realized how much he valued good relationships—friendships included. Once he was able to bring his attention to the present moment at the dinner, he found the sense of connection he so needed with a friend who respected him, and also challenged him to live out what he valued. The experience made him realize again, on a deeper level, how toxic his current intimate relationship was. His disappointment clearly indicated what he valued in relationships: connection, respect, and mutual support. His regret was focused on his loss and distress, rather than on taking action that worked.*

Only in the present moment can you take action that works. By engaging in the present moment in a way that is in accord with what you value, like Derrick, you can enact a response that transforms what is holding you back into action that works for you—rather than against you.

Emotions are poor governors of our lives. They are good employees, but very bad bosses. Emotions like regret are useful indicators of what is wrong, or has gone wrong. They point to possible responses—if you can decipher possibility through the perspective of what you value.

Emotions, bodily sensations, and racing thoughts are all useful information, but they do not offer the wisdom you need to respond in a way that works. Consider this in your own experience.

Is there an internal experience that is taking you away from this present moment? Does it prevent you from taking the steps you need to take? What monster do you need to face to be willing to open up to a valued course of action?

________________________________________________

________________________________________________

________________________________________________

Describe a perspective you can take that enables you to be present in the moment.

________________________________________________

________________________________________________

________________________________________________

Write down the values that enable you to focus on the present moment.

________________________________________________

________________________________________________

Have you noticed any shift in your experience of your story?

________________________________________________

________________________________________________

________________________________________________

________________________________________________

Your contact with the present moment is a precious gift to yourself. It is the moment that contains your most immediate experiences. Expanding your ability and willingness to be present for your life can open everything up. The process of actively contacting your experience of expansion, that part of yourself that is the place of all experience, offers perspectives that reveal what you value. That way, your story and its function can exist without dominating your entire life. You can hold a space for all you experience, and still have more space for more experiences. This is transcendence. It is an expansive state that cannot be fully captured or described.

Through expansion, places where you have been stuck can be transformed. Burdens you have carried can become sources of liberation. The pain you have endured acquires new meaning that transforms your life purpose.

*Malcolm had carried unnecessary burdens regarding guilt about his father's suicide. Now the same age as his father at the time of his death, Malcolm was facing a similar set of circumstances. His marriage was over, he had been fired from his job, and his children were grown and pursuing their lives in distant locations. He felt overwhelmed by a sense of darkness, especially because his life was mirroring his father's.*

*Malcolm knew that he had to make different choices. With meditation practice, he was able to use his breath to focus his attention. He deliberately focused on the sense of darkness that threatened to overwhelm him, imagining that it was like the nighttime side of the planet. He visualized himself lifting out of the room, above the atmosphere, and looking at the earth as a distant satellite. In this expansion, he saw that while the darkness was deep, it was also something that passes. Its cause was temporarily obscured light, caused by the natural turning of the planet. With compassion and kindness, Malcolm allowed himself to grieve what he had lost, then recover from that grief to prepare for the return of the light. When he journaled about this experience, he named the darkness "The Return of Grief." He named the light "The Return of Life." Along the way came a sense of relief, and he felt his burden shift. This shift empowered him to reach out to his children, contact job agencies, and seek the employers he knew needed his skills.*

Consider whether there is a way you could apply this story of expansion to one of your stories or experiences. Try visualizing your burden from far away, possibly from outer space. What perspective or understanding do you gain through a process of expansion or transcendence?

____________________________________________________________

____________________________________________________________

____________________________________________________________

Identify a monster you can view from a different place. How might you rename that experience?

____________________________________________________________

____________________________________________________________

____________________________________________________________

Have you noticed any shifts in your experience of your story? Write them down.

____________________________________________________________

____________________________________________________________

____________________________________________________________

____________________________________________________________

____________________________________________________________

In these exercises, you have been using your values as a reference point for getting unstuck, being accepting and willing, taking perspective, and expanding. Values point to actions that work for your life and its context. Values need to be held with flexibility and a light touch, so you can develop the right response for the current challenges that life throws at you. Doing what you value might still bring you into contact with pain; however, it might be the pain of growth and valued challenges.

When you consider one of your stories or experiences, is there a way you can apply a values-based approach to transforming your experience?

_______________________________________________

_______________________________________________

_______________________________________________

What values do you want to reflect on and apply in a new way?

_______________________________________________

_______________________________________________

_______________________________________________

How might the application of those values change your story?

_______________________________________________

_______________________________________________

_______________________________________________

_______________________________________________

Each of the processes you have been practicing has required you to be committed to taking action that works for you. Each of these skills facilitates engagement with a life that is fulfilling and purposeful. The commitment to taking action is where you can grow through valued challenges.

When you review one of your stories or experiences, what action comes to mind? Write about any action you need to take.

_______________________________________________

_______________________________________________

_______________________________________________

How does the prospect of taking values-based action change your experience of your story?

____________________________________________________________

____________________________________________________________

____________________________________________________________

____________________________________________________________

Each of the processes you have just practiced demonstrates your commitment to values-based action. Well done! All this practice is building skills to free you from toxic responses to your story.

## Responding Freely to Your Inner and Outer World

To free yourself from toxic responses that are poisoning your life, you must drop harsh, critical judgments of your inner and outer world. What you experience may range from freedom and joy to being shut down and in pain. Your response to these worlds may be highly conditioned or totally automatic. Either way, once experienced, your response can be examined with open interest and curiosity.

For example, Charlize is automatically disgusted by the smell of alcohol on someone's breath. If she is dominated by that disgust, and avoids every circumstance where she might encounter that smell, her life will be more limited than she wants it to be. Her disgust is informed by values that support her self-care, protect her from violence, and allow her to avoid distress. However, Charlize also values social interaction with people who like to drink, but who also know how to drink in moderation. While the disgust is based on painful experiences, if it dominates all her social experiences, she will shut down in ways that cut her off from other valued experiences. If Charlize judges herself for her disgust, she will spiral into a thought process that is increasingly bitter, depressing, and anxiety provoking.

Instead, she chose to approach this inner-world experience with openness, interest, and curiosity. She felt compassion for the self that suffered. A balanced approach called for respecting her need for respectful social connection. This balance opened Charlize up to a flexible and adaptable response to this life challenge. This flexibility and adaptability came as a relief from the usual toxic spiral she had experienced in the past.

Only you can observe what you are experiencing in your inner world. However, your behavior is observable to others and, unfortunately, others may judge it despite having no idea what you are experiencing. Charlize's disgust is expressed in her facial expressions and is readily recognized by others. While expressions can be interpreted in many ways, Charlize felt judged and rejected by others as a result. These reactions formed another feedback loop that increased her experience of toxicity. Once she began the process of putting her values into action prior to an event, she was able to be more fully in the present moment—rather than captured by experiences of past pain. Being fully present allowed her to focus on the people she was with and situation she was in, and share experiences with her friends. In this space, she was aware that her friends are responsible people and that she is safe with them. Her sense of safety allowed her to be more relaxed and open to the joys of the moment.

Consider how the stories and experiences you have chosen to work with have been dominating your inner world. Write down an example.

______________________________________________________________________

______________________________________________________________________

______________________________________________________________________

______________________________________________________________________

Write about how this connects to your values. What values might be informing this experience? Does this experience inform your values in some way?

______________________________________________________________________

______________________________________________________________________

______________________________________________________________________

Write about how this inner-world experience might be closing you down to other valued experiences.

______________________________________________

______________________________________________

______________________________________________

Use some of the compassion and perspective skills you have been practicing to open up to more adaptable and flexible responses. What other ways might you respond?

______________________________________________

______________________________________________

______________________________________________

These are key skills that will make your life free, flexible, and values-based. When you move away from what is toxic and poisoning your life, you move toward creating what you value in your life. Sometimes this is easier said than done. Life presents such a range of options for values that are seemingly contradictory. Here is a small sample of seemingly divergent, and sometimes irreconcilable, worldviews.

| Order and Structure | Possibility, Exploration, Chaos |
|---|---|
| Fact | Story/myth/legend |
| Process | Context |
| Focused solutions | Expansive exploration |
| Knowledge | Imagination/intuition |
| Certainty | Mystery |

The left column—order and structure—is how our consciousness tries to simplify our world so that we can function quickly and effectively in typical and predictable circumstances. The right-hand column—possibility, exploration, and chaos—is how our consciousness seeks to move into an unknown and unpredictable future. Both sides are values based, and are effective responses. As long as they are relevant to your current life circumstances, the only criteria for a "right" choice is that the choice works for you.

Like most of us, you have likely had the experience of responding in one way when another way was needed. You may have thought things were predictable, but an unknown factor created chaos. For example, after Lisette began working as a counselor, she was making great progress with a client. Then one day, the client arrived very distressed and Lisette couldn't perceive why. When discussing social situations, her client disclosed that she felt judged for having given up a baby at birth—something she had not revealed. Lisette felt stunned.

On the other hand, you may have thought an exploratory process was called for, but the best response turned out to be an ordered and predictable one. In a new job, Malcolm was asked to create a set of policies for a newly formed department. He used his research skills to look at options, and then he made recommendations for the best policy options that were currently being developed in leading organizations. When it turned out that his boss just wanted him to copy another department's policy, Malcolm felt blindsided.

In both these cases, Lisette and Malcolm were proceeding in seemingly reasonable ways, yet not hitting the mark. Lisette was focused on the predictable, Malcolm was focused on the possible—and the people they were working with wanted the opposite. When this happens, it can be easy to go into a spiral of self-criticism and judgment. All you may have needed to respond effectively was a different approach or set of skills.

Have you had an experience of doing something to the best of your ability, yet being caught unawares by the unexpected? Describe what happened.

________________________________________

________________________________________

________________________________________

If you look at the situation with a compassionate lens, how would you support yourself?

________________________________________

________________________________________

________________________________________

A compassionate lens might help you take a perspective that understands who you were at the time of the experience. Looking back, what do you now understand about yourself and the situation?

___

___

___

Your perspective might reveal what your intentions and needs were, and the unintended effects of your actions or reactions. What does your new perspective reveal about where you were coming from and what happened as a result?

___

___

___

In any pain or struggle, you can uncover hidden values. What values can you see within this experience?

___

___

___

Each experience has a transformative element, perhaps a thought, feeling, or action. What can transform this experience into something workable?

___

___

___

Congratulations on practicing a range of simple, effective skills that are not always easy to apply. With repetition and daily use, they will soon become natural to you. This quick-reference guide to actions that work can help (Harris 2019).

| Actions | Prior Response | Values-Focused Response |
|---|---|---|
| Being accepting and willing to make room for your experience | Pushing down, ignoring, or pushing away distress | Making room for uncomfortable thoughts, feelings, and sensations |
| Being in the present moment | Being anywhere else but here, wishing for different experiences | Taking time to get in touch with what is going on right here and now<br>Taking notice of your breath for three to five minutes |
| Practicing your values | Losing touch with what you value<br>Doing things others demand of you even if these actions are not what you value | Identifying your key values, and considering how you could live more in line with them<br>Ensuring that you have not neglected anything that is important for things that are not important |
| Getting unstuck; defusing your stories | Getting caught by your stories<br>Believing everything your mind tells you | Being consistently mindful of those thoughts that are unworkable<br>Practicing transforming those things that capture you |
| Expanding the observant self | Getting bound up by difficult experiences and the thoughts, feelings, and sensations they automatically generate | Observing your internal experiences without getting bound up in them; asking<br>• How is this like or not like that?<br>• How would another person view this?<br>• How would you see this in five years?<br>• How does this build on or subtract from your values? |
| Taking committed action | Doing things that do not work for you<br>Getting caught by others' agendas | Taking action to live out your values in one key area each day<br>Working on taking a pathway in life that reflects your values |

It can feel easy, and seemingly natural, to fall into old toxic patterns of thinking that poison your life. Each of the exercises in this chapter has challenged you to reflect on how these old patterns have formed in your life. As you have responded to the exercises, you have applied new skills. These skills are essential to forming effective new responses to toxic self-blame, as well as the burdens and internal monsters it creates. These effective responses make a place for these experiences, bringing new perspectives that offer transformative insight into each painful story. Your stories reveal new ways forward in your life, toward outcomes that you truly value. Next, you will be given skills to confirm your experience of self-forgiveness.

CHAPTER 6

# Encounter Self-Forgiveness and Its Responsibilities

In this journey of transformation, you are discovering who you truly are and freeing yourself to fulfill your true meaning and purpose. Encountering your inner monster and transforming your relationship with it, embracing what it has to say, and incorporating all that it has to teach you: this process leads to your treasure. Now it is time to take steps to encounter a deep experience of self-forgiveness and the responsibilities it brings.

Your courage has transformed many of your experiences of pain and suffering. By applying the skills taught in the previous chapters, you benefited from the work of many psychologists who have deeply explored self-compassion. Research has shown the benefit of identifying your points of suffering and bearing witness to them, rather than avoiding them. When you bear witness, you start the process of healing and recovery from pain, suffering, and struggle. Self-forgiveness is the next step.

You are not to blame for random events that may have caused you pain and suffering. What's important in the journey of self-forgiveness is how you may have responded to your experience of those events. Toxic self-blame can get in the way of recovery; for example, if you think, *I was stupid for driving at that time of day when that car hit mine*. Such self-blame can quickly spiral downward, focusing on things that shift your energy away from recovery. There may be no reason that an event happened. Sometimes the only reason that can be found for a random event is the gift of hindsight. Being able to respond in a way that truly reflects your values can free you from toxic self-blame. As you understand your journey of suffering, pain, and healing, you may find an opportunity to help another who experienced a similar misfortune. You may be able to offer the treasure of your journey as a guide to another's recovery.

Consider a lesson you have learned while doing this work. How might you offer this treasure to another person?

_______________________________________________

_______________________________________________

_______________________________________________

_______________________________________________

_______________________________________________

Alternatively, you may have done something that was not in accord with your values. For example, a celebration at your house may have gotten out of control. The late-night noise created conflict between you and a number of your neighbors. The embarrassment of the experience you feel, in the sober light of day, may be an opportunity to hunker down, avoid your neighbors, and let it blow over. But the consequences may be loss of good will. Would that reflect what you truly value?

Your values may be to restore relationships and mend fences, figuratively or perhaps actually. Genuinely apologizing and responding to the hurt caused, perhaps by making restitution, may be needed. It can be painful to face those regrets, to express genuine guilt and remorse, and to take action that your neighbors think is meaningful. However, such an effort may open new ways of communicating and rebuild trust with valued neighbors. Most of all, by doing the external work of dealing with the concerns of the neighborhood, you will have built the basis for engaging in genuine compassion toward yourself and how to deal with your regrets about not acting in accordance with all your values on the big night of celebration. You may find treasure in the process: a new strength or a new view of your integrity. Despite any flaws in your actions, you can make amends in a way that works. You can make a mistake and still grow from it.

Consider any past experiences when something went "wrong," and you needed to make amends. What was the treasure you found?

____________________________________________________________

____________________________________________________________

____________________________________________________________

Whatever your story is, it's worth asking *Why have I gone through this?* For example, Lisette found that her struggles with caring for others were reminders that if she fails to care for herself, she will be unable to truly help others in a way that reflects her values and strengths. Derrick was reminded that a focus on trying to please others leads to relationships that do not work—and that he needs to stay in touch with his values as he dates. Lani found that her crippling criticisms of herself don't lead to self-improvement; instead, they burden her, and remind her to be present and in the moment with herself and her loved ones. Charlize found that her fears around addiction were strangling her instead of protecting her and that she needed to balance them to achieve physical recovery from her injury. Malcolm found that his guilt over his father's death isolated him at a time when he needed to focus on his present-day connections with those he loves.

Each monster has a valid basis that can be a source of learning and reflection when viewed through a compassionate lens. However, each also has the capacity to dominate and distract from living a full and active life, here and now. You can transform and use the energy in each of your stories. They are portals to new treasures. This transformation of your experience is the path that leads to genuine self-forgiveness.

# Open the Door to Genuine Self-Forgiveness

To explore forgiving yourself, identify the life story you have been working on that most dominates and distracts you from engaging in a life you truly value. We will uncover the values your story reveals. Your values are those guiding elements to your inner life that confirm that you are being true to your meaning and purpose. Being true to yourself means that you are able to live with something in good conscience. As an example, here is Lisette's deep reflection on her story and its consequences.

> *While Lisette was learning to care for herself and create boundaries with her demanding family, her thoughts were dominated by the number of times she had not cared for her own welfare. In order to gain perspective, she allowed space for the pain that was overrunning her. She asked this monster, respectfully: "What are you trying to tell me?" The message was clear: "Just because you have asserted yourself once does not mean that you will continue to. Besides, by allowing people to walk over you so many times, you did a lot of damage. So much humiliation. So much pain."*
>
> *Lisette realized that this story pointed toward the work she needed to do to genuinely heal and recover from her many painful experiences. Lisette thanked her monster for revealing this discomfort. In response, she asked for respect from the voice, saying: "I acknowledge that hurt and fear and doubt. Now I need you to let me focus on healing and recovery, rather than on the distress."*

By taking a number of different perspectives on her experience, such as standing beside herself as a friend would, Lisette shifted from being critical to being concerned and supportive. She found that she valued being constructive and expansive when responding to her challenges. The lesson that revealed itself to Lisette was that she needed to explore and build on the values and actions that worked for her health and her whole self.

Now think about your most dominating and distracting story. In what way did this story try to protect you?

______________________________________________________________________

______________________________________________________________________

______________________________________________________________________

______________________________________________________________________

Describe how this story no longer serves you. What are the ways it distracts or dominates you?

______________________________________________________________________

______________________________________________________________________

______________________________________________________________________

______________________________________________________________________

Now look at this story from different points of view. What does a compassionate lens reveal? An expansive view? Write down your observations.

______________________________________________________________________

______________________________________________________________________

______________________________________________________________________

______________________________________________________________________

______________________________________________________________________

Reflect on how these different perspectives change your experience of the story. For example, does an alternate emotion arise? Does a physical sensation alter? Does a new way of considering it arise? Does an attitude shift?

What does this change reveal about your values?

Why have you gone through this experience? Write about its lessons for you.

What values does your story now reflect?

Genuine self-forgiveness requires that you clarify a genuine need before you can formulate a substantial response. Your work on your needs will give you a template for how to develop values-based responses to life challenges that have previously dominated and distracted you.

One technique is to use OPAL, an acronym that stands for openness, presence, acceptance, and light. It is a meditative process that can help you hold your experience of your needs. Find a safe, quiet place. Initially focus on your breathing, and prepare to take a break if the experience is overwhelming. Then focus your attention on your experience with the following stances:

**Openness:** Allow all your experience to be as it is—the pain, the lessons, the need for change, whatever arises. Let it present itself to you, free from any harsh or critical judgment.

**Presence:** As you allow the totality of your experience, be present with it. Feel the emotions, sense the physical sensations, be aware of your thoughts. That way, you do not reject, hide, or ignore any of it.

**Acceptance:** Take an attitude of acceptance. Your experience is what it is. Your painful story was what it was. There is no room for resignation or tolerance; instead accept your experience.

**Light:** Imagine that your awareness of your experience is a candle or flashlight. Bring light to dark places by becoming curious about what is there. Your interest in yourself can reveal hidden messages, and bring a sense of lightening the heaviness of your previous experience.

*Charlize allowed room for all her experience, including the chronic pain of her condition, the fear of addiction, her frustrations with her family, and her loss of belief in her future. The most prominent experience was a deep sense of shame about her family's addiction story. She had used that shame as a way to protect herself from rejection. In particular, until using OPAL, she had refused to think about her own deep need to start a family, as she was too afraid of being rejected by a partner who could not tolerate her distress about alcohol and addiction. If she was to respond to this deep need, she must stop punishing herself for her family story, and address her fear of rejection.*

Is there an experience you need to hold using OPAL? Write it down.

_______________________________________________

_______________________________________________

_______________________________________________

Try the OPAL meditation. Then describe your experience applying it.

_______________________________________________

_______________________________________________

_______________________________________________

_______________________________________________

_______________________________________________

What deep needs were revealed?

_______________________________________________

_______________________________________________

_______________________________________________

Once you are aware of your needs, you can begin taking genuine responsibility for meeting them. It may be helpful to create a mantra for yourself. A mantra is something you repeat to yourself as an encouraging reminder of what you are learning to integrate into your life. When Lani confronted her bullying inner monster, who was constantly persecuting her with criticism, she found a personal mantra that could calm that voice down: *Life is not happening "to" me. Life is happening "for" me.*

A personal mantra can enable new perspective on your life challenges. With it, you can approach your challenges as opportunities to grow as a person. This new perspective is the value of taking responsibility. It can replace responses of toleration and resignation, and the feeling of being persecuted by life setbacks. When you identify the key you need, in the form of a personal mantra, to open yourself to acting on your values, you gain a new way to navigate life. The very needs you were previously avoiding and destructively responding to become your guiding light.

Write down at least one personal mantra you can use as a reminder of what you need.

_______________________________________________

_______________________________________________

*Lani felt thankful for the seemingly toxic responses because, at the time, they worked to keep her alive. It wasn't her best life, but she was alive. Lani thanked this monster kindly for providing survival responses. However, Lani then informed her monster: "I am letting these responses go, as they no longer serve me. Now I can open a doorway to become the person I am evolving into."*

Did your inner monster protect you, like Lani's did? Express your gratitude for that protection. Then find a way of letting the monster know it is time to move on to a new approach.

_______________________________________________

_______________________________________________

_______________________________________________

_______________________________________________

_______________________________________________

You are now in touch with your needs. You have taken responsibility for your own life. And you have expressed your desire to move forward in your own way. Still, once something is seen, it can never be unseen. Once something is learned, it can never be unlearned. So how can you forgive yourself when you continue to carry these challenging burdens?

To forgive is to make something as it was before. There is a way to do this. While it sounds simple, it is not easy to put into practice. You must find a way to drop the judgments you make of yourself for what you have heard, seen, experienced, and known. Dropping judgment will allow you to begin the process of learning new experiences of yourself, which allow you to focus on a values-informed life that reflects your true meaning and purpose.

# Getting Playful with Experiences

In the OPAL process, you are encouraged to bring lightness to meditations on your experience. One of the ways to do this is to bring a sense of playfulness to aspects of your journey, furthering the process of transformative storytelling. In your imagination, you can engage your monster any way you choose. So why not bring some humor into the situation? If this sounds challenging, here are some ways others have done it.

- Derrick played a game with the monster, telling it to keep everyone pleased and happy all the time. In his imagination, Derrick lined up everyone he had to please in front of his monster. Then he demanded that his monster try to please every one of those people. After only a few encounters with all their conflicting "must dos," his monster became exasperated and exhausted. Derrick clearly saw how living according to his values, and not others' values, was the only way he could live a life that worked.

- Lisette imagined how, in order to serve the needs of others, she had broken herself into many parts. She visualized herself as a jigsaw puzzle. Then she made a game of identifying each piece and bringing them all together. Once the puzzle was assembled, she saw that she was bigger than even the picture on the jigsaw. She realized that if she brought her whole self into difficult moments, she could respond to her family challenges in new, creative ways.

- Lani gave each of her crippling criticisms a different personality and, in her imagination, put them in a room together. Instead of criticizing her, they argued about which of them was the most important. When absolute bedlam broke out, she knew that these monsters could never guide her in ways that worked. She closed the door of that room and imagined them arguing themselves to exhaustion. Then she went back into the room and said, "Each of you has something valid to say. But from now on, I will listen only when you can say things with respect."

- As part of her postoperative recovery, Charlize imagined her fears as an evil puppet master pulling her strings and getting her to dance to a tune that was not hers. She then imagined that her experience of healing was like a big pair of scissors. She cut those strings and liberated herself. Then she could be her true self, focused on her life purpose, rather than focused on fear.

- Malcolm dropped judgment of himself and his father, and started meditating on a conversation of mutual love and support with his father. They focused on the terrific things that his father's grandchildren and great-grandchildren were doing. As they traded stories of antics, youthful mistakes, and tremendous achievements, Malcolm saw that there is humor and laughter in the shared experience of parenthood.

Now describe a part of your story that you can bring this sense of lightness to.

_______________________________________________

_______________________________________________

_______________________________________________

_______________________________________________

_______________________________________________

_______________________________________________

_______________________________________________

Is there a humorous way to transform things? Can you turn your relationship with a monster into a game? Describe how you will bring lightness into the story.

_______________________________________________

_______________________________________________

_______________________________________________

_______________________________________________

_______________________________________________

What does looking at the situation in a lighter way show you?

______________________________________________________________________

______________________________________________________________________

______________________________________________________________________

______________________________________________________________________

______________________________________________________________________

You have done so well to arrive at this place. You have built a broad set of skills! Now you are ready to choose self-forgiveness, so let's take the next step.

## Deciding to Forgive Your Self

On this journey of transformation, your values are your guide to self-forgiveness that works. As you have seen, within each of your experiences is an indicator of your values. These experiences include what you see in a black mirror of potentially horrible events, seemingly destructive situations, and any ways you have failed to implement your known values. Consider these accounts of self-forgiveness.

- Derrick decided to forgive the part of himself that tried to please others. He acknowledged that pleasing others was an important, but misguided, focus. He acknowledged that part of himself was undermining his own need for a values-informed relationship that reflected his whole self, and was therefore causing pain. With self-forgiveness, Derrick embraced his whole self and appreciated the ongoing journey of discovery and growth.
- Lisette decided to embrace the monster that constantly criticized her for not doing all she "needed" to do for her family. As a result, she acknowledged that family was a core value for her, and also that her family must accept her need for self-care. Her monster apologized for having impossible standards that were hurtful and damaging. In forgiving herself, Lisette dropped harsh critical judgment of herself—on both sides of this experience—and felt clarity and stillness.

- Lani faced a monster that she had named "I am broken." Through the process of transforming her story, she saw that her life actually revealed that she was strong and could mend in mind and body. Further, she saw how her struggles made her who she was: a kinder, more compassionate person. Her journey made her less of a perfectionist and more able to connect with those she loved at a deep, visceral level. She was able to thank and embrace her monster, as it had helped her discover an inner voice that said, "I am whole." In this state, she could truly forgive herself.
- Charlize acknowledged that her fear of addiction had been a huge burden, yet an important part of avoiding the traps of substance use. After a respectful discussion with her monster, they agreed this stance was important, but excessive. Her monster released her to live a full and active life, knowing Charlize could live sober and healthy. Charlize's self-forgiveness allowed her to physically recover and seek the intimate relationship that she valued.
- Malcolm thanked the monster that had shamed him for his father's suicide. He acknowledged that it helped him survive many life setbacks that had been similar to the ones his father had experienced. He forgave himself for "neglecting" his family by acknowledging the many ways he had supported them. What he had done was more important than what he could have done. He resolved to use the energy previously absorbed by shame to do things he valued.

Consider these examples. Identify the elements of your story that indicate your values. Then find the focus of your self-forgiveness. What do you need to forgive yourself for?

______________________________________________________________________

______________________________________________________________________

______________________________________________________________________

______________________________________________________________________

______________________________________________________________________

______________________________________________________________________

Describe any part of you that needs to be acknowledged, embraced, and transformed.

___

___

___

Express your forgiveness toward yourself in a way that is meaningful to you.

___

___

___

Along the way, has there been a discovery that indicates the pathway to your true calling? If so, write it down.

___

___

___

___

___

Self-forgiveness is a process, not a destination. Your experience of common humanity means that this skill will be one you can call on over and over again. You can fine-tune and direct your life pathway anytime you want, to fulfill your meaning and purpose.

Different aspects of your monster or inner critic may reveal themselves at different points in your experience, perhaps in the form of a passing reminder or, alternatively, making you see things in a new light. Whatever your experience, all the skills you have learned and applied so far can be used to continue your journey of healing and fulfillment.

# Reinforcing Your Transformation

Here is a meditation on experiencing fears that may arise as you progress. Some call these fears relapsing, and others see them as revisiting old patterns. At http://www.newharbinger.com/45694, you can download a copy of this meditation to use throughout your life. There are several questions you can respond to either on the blank lines provided here or on the download itself. A guided audio recording of this meditation is also available.

*Fears tell us what we are not, or what we do not want.*

*Fears are a black mirror of who we are and might be.*

*The answer to fear?*

*When a fear is felt, imaged, dreamed, thought, or experienced in any way—make room for it.*

*Observe what is revealed.*

*Suspend harsh, critical judgment. Turn toward curiosity and openness, with love, and embrace whatever comes up with warmth and acceptance.*

What are these fears telling you? Write down the messages.

________________________________________

________________________________________

________________________________________

________________________________________

What are these fears trying to protect?

________________________________________

________________________________________

________________________________________

Now name the entity that is being protected, whether it is a part of your self, your past, an inner monster, or an outdated sense of who you are.

___

Take some time to engage in the OPAL process with this entity: openness, presence, acceptance, light.

If this entity was strong and capable, what would it look like?

___

___

What would it achieve?

___

___

What would that feel like?

___

___

What experiences could you explore further?

___

___

With these perspectives, how might that entity behave in the presence of what was feared?

___

___

___

If that entity were allowed to be all it could be, what would it look like after two years had passed? Five years?

________________________________________________________________________________

________________________________________________________________________________

________________________________________________________________________________

________________________________________________________________________________

________________________________________________________________________________

Now consider what your experience would be like if, in response to your fear, you expressed one of the following values-based affirmations:

*I am powerful.*

*I am worthy.*

*I am wanted for who I am.*

*I am protected.*

*I am assertive.*

*I am loved.*

*I am strong.*

*I am attractive.*

Meditate on one of these values-based affirmations. Notice again what arises as you meditate on this affirmation with openness, interest, and curiosity. Write down what you experience.

________________________________________________________________________________

________________________________________________________________________________

________________________________________________________________________________

________________________________________________________________________________

________________________________________________________________________________

What has changed through that experience of fear? What actions do you need to take in your life to best reflect this change?

________________________________________________________________________________

The steps you have taken can powerfully transform your existence. The process of self-forgiveness can shift your world on its axis. Why? You now see so many things in a new light and can therefore act in new ways when troublesome old patterns, experiences, people, places, and challenges arise. The coming chapters offer a guide to embedding what you have learned so far into a new approach to living a life informed by deep meaning and purpose.

CHAPTER 7

# Build a New Way Forward Based on Self-Forgiveness

You are encountering the mystery behind the journey of self-forgiveness. It is a mystery because you can never quite know where this journey of discovery will lead. You are unique—no one will ever have your experience, your journey, or a complete understanding of who you are. What you learn on this journey is uniquely yours. While you may want to make things as they were before, you will never be in exactly the same place again. Time changes places, people, and circumstances both subtly and drastically. Instead, through self-forgiveness, you now have the opportunity to experience new freedom of action, a sense of wonder, and challenges to learn from.

Just as every mistake, setback, and life challenge has within it the opportunity to learn, innovate, and overcome, every solution has challenges, pitfalls, and decisions (Harris 2006). Recall any New Year's resolutions you may have made. At the time, you probably had great resolve to implement them, but there were likely obstacles to sustaining that desired change. It takes work to change all the factors that support a resolution. In the same way, on the path to self-forgiveness, it helps to prepare for valued change to sustain it.

That is why self-forgiveness is not a destination; it is a skill to be constantly called upon, practiced, experimented with, and implemented. Any difficulties you face, including the repetition of challenges, are lessons in practicing what you have learned about yourself. Every step could instigate further pain, suffering, and struggle (Harris 2011). However, each step also offers a renewed opportunity to practice empathy, understanding, and love toward the you that is having the experience. Hardship and adversity contain opportunities for deep learning. Challenging experiences strengthen your responses by testing what works for you.

Others who have taken the journey you are now on have described the process as a "spiral journey." It is as if they steadily climbed a mountain by ascending slowly, taking a circular pathway that lifted them with each circuit. The path often took them close to previous experiences, but each time they had a different vantage point (Harris 2012).

Here's how Derrick reflected on the path he took, after he ended a relationship that his family supported, but was not in accord with his values for open, exploratory, vulnerable communication.

*Derrick was able to forgive himself for the pain of his inaction by learning what he really was seeking in relationship. He took time to heal. Then Derrick sought a new relationship based on shared values. Once the initial good vibes, or the honeymoon phase, passed, he realized that it took work to actually communicate, be vulnerable, truly open up to someone. Sometimes the effort to deal with misunderstanding still caused pain. He feared repeating what had happened in his old relationship. However, what had changed was that his new partner was equally willing to invest work in communicating authentically and learning from the vulnerability of their mutual challenges. At this point, Derrick revisited his self-forgiveness work and understood that even in relationships that work well, pain and suffering may arise. The difference this time was that healing and restoration followed.*

*His decisions created distance and tension with his family. They were uncomfortable with his going against cultural norms about marriage and relationship. Derrick revisited an important lesson: he could not change others. Instead, he put energy into his new relationship, as he valued it more than cultural norms. However, this shift in focus brought up deep, unexpected emotions. He became very angry with his family. When he made room for this new emotion, Derrick realized this anger was a combination of disappointment that they did not appreciate the suffering he had experienced trying to please them, and feeling foolish that he had tried to please them at all. Their snarky comments showed that they were fixated upon appearances and saving face. Once again, Derrick did self-forgiveness work on these unexpected emotional states and the experience of rejection by others.*

*There was also an experience of shame, as Derrick feared that he couldn't be the person his partner expected. By calling upon his value of openness in relationships, they engaged in deep conversations about these struggles. Their shared humanity and vulnerability allowed them to grow and discover new aspects of each other and themselves. They set regular times to explore these experiences, which made room for Derrick to continue being actively engaged with self-forgiveness as a tool for new steps, directions, and challenges. Derrick and his partner shared their experiences with friends and family who were willing to listen and understand their journey with openness and curiosity.*

Let's explore what your pathway may look like. You may have some of these elements, they may occur in a different order, or you may consider preparing strategies for when they arise. Here are elements of the ongoing pathway of self-forgiveness.

Write about one realization you have had that change is required because something is wrong in your life.

What did you discover as a result of that new realization? Note what has changed in your view of your experience.

You encounter loss and its consequences. Write about this loss and all it reveals for you.

You may experience darkness and heaviness. Can you embrace this? What message might this experience give you about your journey?

Can you accept, make room, and allow a process of transformation? What shifts in this process as you do this?

___

___

___

By understanding that there is a process of learning and incorporating changes, your values become clearer. Identify what you value that points toward action you need to take in your life.

___

___

___

___

You consistently start to overcome what was going wrong by taking action that works. Name the actions you are taking based on your values.

___

___

___

You forgive yourself for whatever story you carried about yourself, and the consequences of following it. What is it you are forgiving?

___

___

___

Because you must live in the world, with family, friends, workplace, or neighborhood that does not necessarily understand or appreciate your valued change, consider what barriers you might face. How could you manage those challenges?

_______________________________________________

_______________________________________________

_______________________________________________

_______________________________________________

_______________________________________________

When you incorporate these consequences of change, you can draw on the skills in this workbook. What are two things you have learned that will support your ongoing journey?

_______________________________________________

_______________________________________________

_______________________________________________

_______________________________________________

Unexpected responses arise, both internally and externally. What further experiences have you noticed on this pathway of change?

_______________________________________________

_______________________________________________

_______________________________________________

_______________________________________________

You may find that friends no longer understand you, while unexpected people do. How can you make room for these experiences?

______________________________________________

______________________________________________

______________________________________________

______________________________________________

As you make decisions on how to live with this new state of responding to the world, you need to maintain these changes. How will you live in a new way that reflects your values?

______________________________________________

______________________________________________

______________________________________________

______________________________________________

Passing your lessons on to others supports your journey. What lesson could others learn from your journey?

______________________________________________

______________________________________________

______________________________________________

______________________________________________

Let's continue to reflect on common lessons people share about their life journey when they start to apply the skills of self-forgiveness as they forge a new way forward in life.

# Threads of Fear

Fear of rejection, embarrassment, shame, and so on, can be what keeps us stuck in patterns that have not worked. Fear has a valid basis, keeping you safe and vigilant about the risks of harm. By making room for the basis of this fear, self-forgiveness can bring love, acceptance, and safety to that fearful self.

*Madelyn feared that her children wouldn't love her if she were not with them 100 percent of the time, experiencing and sharing in everything they lived through. She identified this feeling as a fear of missing out. After she forgave herself for separating from their father and dropped the harsh, critical self-judgment that came with her fear, she was able to direct her attention clearly. She actually found her children appreciated her even more because their time together was limited. Her absence made them realize what she had to offer as a mother, and they didn't take that for granted. They appreciated what each parent offered as an individual: their dad fostered adventure, challenge, and independence; Madelyn focused on talking about feelings and life challenges. The children also built resilience and fostered deeper bonds as siblings.*

Consider what fears may be being released in the pathway you are following. What is revealed by looking at your fear?

______________________________________________________________________

______________________________________________________________________

______________________________________________________________________

______________________________________________________________________

______________________________________________________________________

______________________________________________________________________

# Energy Release

Self-forgiveness releases you from patterns of self-destruction that are energy absorbing. You now have the opportunity to redirect that energy toward what you value. Practicing and applying theses skills brings profound changes. Getting unhooked from constant self-criticism allows for so much more space and energy for thinking, feeling, acting, and growing on all levels—emotional, physical, and spiritual. It can all be applied to what you really want to focus on.

*After Lisette released herself from her critical inner voice and healed the hurt of family gatherings that had not worked, she focused on creating gatherings that did work for her benefit as well as those who attended. She joined more informal events outside the standard holidays, birthdays, and anniversaries, events where they could focus on just being in each other's company and sharing fun. When her first event was over, she was physically tired but emotionally charged that she had acted according to her values.*

Write about what you might want to focus released energy on—something you value.

_______________

_______________

_______________

_______________

_______________

_______________

# Meaning and Purpose Produce Growth and Learning

A life based on values, in pursuit of your meaning and purpose, continues to be a journey of growth and learning. Why is this so? You have a unique meaning that is yours and yours alone. Getting familiar with self-forgiveness allows you to take risks that help you live in ways that fulfill your meaning and purpose. The unique elements of who you are—your DNA, your experience, your memories, all you have learned, and the values you have formed—give you the totality of what drives meaning in your life. Your purpose is to fulfill that meaning and, if you are called, to share and teach others. However, even if you act in a way that is totally informed by your values and in pursuit of meaning, you will still make mistakes and miss the mark on occasions. Self-forgiveness takes away the unnecessary criticism and helps you use all the skills you have learned to grow in through experience.

*Before she entered the pathway of self-forgiveness, Charlize had a deep belief that she was broken. Her journey showed her that she was not the story of her family. She was instead a strong, independent woman who, despite her pain, had deep reserves of strength. This strength could deeply mend both her body and mind. Her struggles informed a sense of purpose: to be a kinder, more compassionate, more humane person. She did not need a perfect life to be a loving partner and parent of healthy, happy children. At a deep, visceral layer of her being, she knew her purpose was to break the cycle of family dysfunction and addiction in the way she lived her life by raising her own family.*

Consider your life meaning and the purpose your pathway is revealing to you. What learning and growth are opening up to you?

_______________________________________________

_______________________________________________

_______________________________________________

_______________________________________________

_______________________________________________

# Cultivating Openness

Pursuing your life meaning and purpose is facilitated by openness to alternate decisions, putting aside critical harsh judgments, and dropping black-and-white views. This openness is created through seeking different perspectives in order to understand alternative viewpoints you can take.

> *When Lani began to be curious about her harsh, critical inner voice, she used a wry sense of humor. She named this voice "Lies I told myself." The big lies were "I'm no good with money" and "I'm not organized." Using openness with a sense of fun and joy, she then sifted through each alternative viewpoint of her life, and found that she was really good at keeping receipts and managing her taxes. She had lived well on a student income. She was great at saving. By applying for great jobs, she had traveled the world. She was known at her work for running great record-keeping systems, and people relied on her. By being open to her story, treating it with humor, and considering an alternate view of herself, Lani was able to move toward a different perspective of herself that was liberating.*

Write about how cultivating openness, particularly seasoned with humor, might help you adopt a new viewpoint.

______________________________________________

______________________________________________

______________________________________________

______________________________________________

______________________________________________

# Refining Your Values

By engaging in the work of genuine self-forgiveness, you can continually refine how you align your intentions, values, and actions in the face of life challenges. Reflecting on those decisions can reveal lessons on how to take values-informed actions that work.

*With openness, interest, and curiosity, Lisette wondered what values were behind the inner critic. She found that she highly valued the capacity to do her job well. Her "not good enough" story was a mutated version of ensuring that she was competent and genuinely providing a high-quality service. The "seeking approval" story was a deeply wounded version of the need to be connected and valued by those she loved.*

*She created a checklist for ongoing professional development and set up an additional round of peer support at her workplace, to check in on her ongoing professional performance. The "seeking approval" story made Lisette feel unsafe when she expanded to make room for the experience of being ignored. In a guided meditation, she felt the sense of being abandoned and shamed. Her basic values that were not being met were connection and true confidence in herself as a whole and worthy person. She thanked the critic for revealing these values, and put together a plan to connect with people she deeply trusted to discuss these needs. She was then able to forgive that part of herself that held on to those stories in a bid to misguidedly protect her.*

Write about how refining your values can be helped by exploring hard experiences.

______________________________________________________________________

______________________________________________________________________

______________________________________________________________________

______________________________________________________________________

______________________________________________________________________

# Releasing the Capacity to Love

Self-forgiveness releases our capacity to love ourselves, our partners, families, communities, and the greater creation that surrounds us. The focus on your inner monster can trap you in self-loathing, self-hatred, and other emotions that reject who you are. This entrapment is often driven by feeling that you are not meeting social standards, failing to meet what you think you should be, and losing touch with your own values. These feelings put you in a place where you are being caught by other agendas, and likely lead you to being caught in spirals of self-reinforcing internal criticisms. The deep work of self-forgiveness breaks these cycles and restores love for yourself, which brings a greater capacity to release love for others.

*Malcolm realized that he didn't need to focus on guilt and shame that he had made so many wrong choices. With the benefit of compassionate hindsight, he realized that he made the best choices he was aware of at the time he made them. These decisions had allowed him to survive, and each step was an opportunity to slowly grow. He wanted to give himself the love that he felt his father's death had stripped from him.*

*He thanked the vulnerable younger version of himself for being brave in facing the turmoil of his youth. He then turned to the older version who had offered the younger version forgiveness, and thanked him for becoming a fearless, open-hearted person who was open to new experiences and love, and full of kindness to others. By being consistently kind to himself, he felt that sense of love for the person he now was and had become through enduring all that pain and hardship. The experiences he endured guided his growth into the person he had become. As heat and pressure forge diamonds from a lump of coal, now was the time to allow Malcolm's inner beauty to shine on those he loved and cherished.*

Write about how applying these skills may release love in your life, either toward yourself, to others, or to the wider creation.

___

___

___

# Decisions and New Places

Self-forgiveness teaches that all decisions have consequences that take you to new places. You have seen that taking a variety of perspectives on a problem can provide novel and unexpected solutions. Each of those solutions then brings interesting, varied, and sometime unexpected challenges. A common experience on the pathway of healing hovers around an unexpected set of regrets, including *Why didn't I do this before?* or *My life would have been so different if I had done this when…* You may have many more regrets. A key to renewal is to drop the expectation of easiness and understand that growth enables you to exercise and build your engagement with values, and practice new skills.

*When Charlize fully recovered from her surgeries, she was grateful for the skills and expertise of her surgeons and physical therapists. She got through her pain relief without a hint of dependence and was initially elated at how well she recovered and was functioning.*

*However, after a month or so she felt deeply self-critical about why she had taken so long to get the surgery. She revisited previous meditations on her fears. With compassion and empathy, she held that fearful part of herself in a soft embrace and assured her that all was now well. She could look toward her next major fear around relationships, as she was afraid of being rejected by a partner for the addiction in her family. Charlize was able to lean into her reservations and allow a sense of discomfort as she took action. She began exploring a deeper relationship with someone who had been patiently waiting for her to resolve her health issues. She thanked the story of fear and its regrets, and the action it had now prompted. She found that the connection with her new partner was better than she could have hoped for.*

Consider how decisions you make that are informed by your values, meaning, and purpose may take you to new places. Name some directions or places you may move toward.

________________________________________

________________________________________

________________________________________

What challenges might you then need to explore?

## Applying What You Have Learned

The next exercise asks you to revisit each of the unique life challenges presented to you so far. Think of a current challenge you are facing, and then apply each of the lessons you have learned so far. This exercise may take some time to complete. Work slowly and carefully through each question.

Write down your current challenge.

Take time to be present with it—what are your reflections?

What is the power in the story?

_______________

_______________

_______________

What are the choices that have presented themselves, including those that seem irreconcilable?

_______________

_______________

_______________

How are you exiled from this story? Is there a need to embrace it?

_______________

_______________

_______________

What happens when you make room for this story and any pain or suffering it raises?

_______________

_______________

_______________

How are you navigating the challenges in these exercises?

_______________

_______________

_______________

Now let's apply a compassionate lens.

Describe how you are being compassionate toward yourself as you confront your pain and suffering.

______________________________________________

______________________________________________

______________________________________________

How does your compassionate approach transform your perspective on your experience?

______________________________________________

______________________________________________

______________________________________________

Describe the transformation you are making from a response that is not healthy to a response that is healthy.

______________________________________________

______________________________________________

______________________________________________

Now let's take a different perspective on your story. Remember to hold any discomfort you experience with a sense of compassion.

What new perspective can you take?

______________________________________________

______________________________________________

______________________________________________

What does this new perspective reveal?

______________________________

______________________________

______________________________

Is there a particular monster that is revealed?

______________________________

______________________________

______________________________

What do you discover? Are there alternate stories or an opportunity for transformation?

______________________________

______________________________

______________________________

It's time to explore transformational experiences.

What has your journey and responses revealed about your values?

______________________________

______________________________

______________________________

What values do you need to respond to and take action on?

______________________________

______________________________

______________________________

What steps will you take to put your values into action?

______________________________________________

______________________________________________

______________________________________________

You can free yourself from the poison in your life. Here's how.

Identify at least three actions that work to change your previous responses to this story.

Action 1 ______________________________________________

______________________________________________

______________________________________________

Action 2 ______________________________________________

______________________________________________

______________________________________________

Action 3 ______________________________________________

______________________________________________

______________________________________________

It's time to forgive yourself.

What is the hidden treasure, or what you can actually gain, in your story?

______________________________________________

______________________________________________

______________________________________________

Describe how you are applying OPAL (openness, presence, acceptance, light) to your experience.

______

______

______

How will you step into self-forgiveness?

______

______

______

Now look at the new way forward you have learned.

What are the key lessons that give you a new way forward in your life?

______

______

______

# Claiming Your Authentic Self

By engaging with this work, you are preparing yourself for the next stage of your life. You are stepping toward claiming your authentic self. You have identified so many challenges that life has thrown you. You have worked to apply the benefits and manage the drawbacks of the way you previously responded. By nurturing your authentic self, you are becoming more fully aware that the story that you should always be happy and functional is just a story. Instead, your authentic life is guided by your meaning and purpose. In turn, this guidance fulfills your unique potential.

You have been able to transform both helpful and unhelpful stories. You have given yourself insight and practical assistance based on your values to do what is most useful for you. Even those stories that set you up for past failure, and that were destructive, can now be transformed into new places to find treasure through the skills of self-forgiveness.

You have used skills of observation and perspective taking to examine your experience and story. To do this, you have cultivated the sense of being the experiencer of all you experience. You have used the skills of self-compassion to open up and make room for hard-won lessons. Through being open, interested, and curious, you have embraced your monsters and transformed the power and place they hold within you. You have practiced and applied a number of skills to free yourself from being stuck in old patterns of moving away from, or toward, events in a way that was not guided by your values. You now have a deeper understanding of the variety of values that inform your responses to life, and you have put together these skills to take meaningful, purposeful action that aligns with your values.

These skills are your companions on your life's journey to fulfil your personal calling. Ironically, your inner critic or your monster may have been the greatest initial clue to that calling. You have experienced how self-forgiveness is a catalyst to transform your relationship with that monster. This transformation is the key to the journey toward the difference you are called to make to this world.

Your heart calls you to live an authentic life and make the unique contribution only you can make to this world. Next a challenge awaits you...

CHAPTER 8

# Share What You Have Learned with Others

While no one else will ever live exactly the way you have, your lessons can teach about challenges many of us have in common. You have the opportunity to share your authentic self and give inspiration to others. You can give others the means to gain insight more quickly and effectively than you have, releasing them to make their unique contribution with greater skill and power than they might have without your assistance. Through sharing your discovery with others, you have the ability to multiply its benefits.

There may be an individual, a family, a social community, or coworkers who would benefit from learning about your sacred journey to your authentic life. You have been engaging with your meaning and purpose at deeper and more practical levels, and these benefits can transcend your individual experience. As you hold your story lightly and use perspective-taking to expand, heighten, and deepen your learning, you are ready to share the experience. Sharing with others renews your own openness, interest, and curiosity. Your experience broadens by including the perspectives of others. In this way, the journey continues to widen the scope of your leaning. By sharing your treasure, you are constructing scaffolding for the next stage of emotional well-being on your authentic life journey.

You can free others to engage in their own journeys of discovery, liberation, and healing. Storytelling is a deep way of bonding with others and passing on learning and experience. The process of self-forgiveness allows you to not only share the best of your experience but also to transform the darkest parts of your stories and give them new light and meaning. Your journey to authenticity becomes a unique and captivating adventure. You too can transform what was previously a deeply held experience of inner rejection and shame into your own heroic journey.

By transforming your story through self-forgiveness, you can give to others what they may crave, a superhero story they can relate to. Hollywood builds a metaverse of superheroes, each with their own compelling story of overcoming their own inner demons or monsters and then transforming their world. Likewise, you now have an engaging, powerful tale of transforming your experience of adversity. When you tell a relatable story that others can engage with, you re-experience your journey through the eyes and ears of others by sharing a vivid and engaging recounting of your journey toward your authentic life. The heroic journey is a powerful tool for communication. However, unless a story is shared, it has no power. Consider one part of your experience that may help another avoid or overcome pitfalls.

With respect and holding your experience with openness, presence, acceptance, and light, consider one of your dark experiences. Recount it with lightness and humor, as if you were sharing it with a trusted friend.

______________________________________________

______________________________________________

______________________________________________

______________________________________________

______________________________________________

______________________________________________

Storytelling is so powerful because humans have a shared experience of transformation. In this sharing process, the transformation is multiplied from one person to two people to possibly thousands or perhaps even billions. Once a story is shared, it has the opportunity to become part of the whole, whether it be with your partner, your family, your friendship group, community, or the wider society.

If you consider this challenge daunting, you may think you have no right to speak with authority. But you may equally consider your right to not share that which may be of benefit to others. Neither of these rights is absolute and of course they need to be balanced; nevertheless, consider sharing in the context of your values. What will give the greatest benefit in your life and the lives of those you share your story with?

Identify any values you have around helping others, or relating to them. Write them down.

______________________________________________

______________________________________________

______________________________________________

Consider how sharing the lessons you have learned on this journey might be a values-based action. Write about the meaning and purpose that may result.

____________________________________________________________

____________________________________________________________

____________________________________________________________

____________________________________________________________

____________________________________________________________

As you explore your story more deeply with others, you consolidate how it sits in your internal universe of values. Your inner critic and the monsters you have faced may have caused you to hide deeply within the pain and suffering of your experience. These bothersome companions have likely silenced you. The story of your journey may need to be liberated to transform the way you think about your world, the opinions you express, and the lessons you have learned.

> *Madelyn challenged herself to not repeat previous mistakes with her new partner. She was determined to refine her story and share it with her partner. She was able to share key transformations about how she had shut herself down in previous toxic experiences, and how she now opened up to living her authentic life. By sharing her story, she could challenge and engage her partner to see if they were on a similar pathway of growth and development.*

As you have courageously faced experiences that reminded you of distress and dark experiences, you have been navigating triggering experiences. You have learned how to turn toward, and embrace, a trigger in order to transform it through examining it and engaging with its inherent values. What may have previously been traumatizing is now a place where you grow. In sharing your story, you extend your experience of healing and growth by allowing others to either enter into their own journey of healing, or perhaps helping them avoid the pitfalls you fell into. By releasing what has been previously suppressed by your inner critic, a beneficial new universe can reach you and others.

*Malcolm engaged with community groups that were assisting families that had experienced loss. He was able to transform what had previously been shameful for him. By helping others discuss their distress, he could let them know they were not alone. Then he could share that there is a way through distress to a new life that is productive and valuable.*

This process of connection will allow you to create a space in which others can not only reflect on your story but also begin applying the skills that have brought you to where you are now. This connection is a place of true respect. By sharing perspective and your authentic biographical experience, you have a deep capacity to connect at an emotional level. In turn, this connection can grip another person's thinking and challenge them to consider new ways to view their life story, which can either affirm or change their views about how they see themselves and their life.

*Sophie had always felt like she was alone in her struggles. She thought that nobody could possibly understand the experience of chronic pain she had gone through. But that all changed when she met Charlize. Charlize had a way of making Sophie feel heard and understood. When Charlize shared her own story of overcoming struggles, it was as if a light had been switched on for Sophie. For the first time, Sophie felt like she wasn't alone in her pain. Charlize had created a safe space for Sophie to reflect on her own story and allowed her to begin applying the skills she had learned on her own journey.*

*Charlize's vulnerability and authenticity created a deep emotional connection with Sophie that challenged her to view her own struggles in a new light. Sophie began to see herself as someone who was capable of living in a new way. Over time, Sophie's perspective shifted. She was inspired by Charlize's strength and resilience through her journey of transformation through self-forgiveness. Now she had a newfound sense of purpose and direction, and was practicing the lessons Charlize had learned. Charlize's connection with Sophie created a safe place to see her own story in a new light.*

Is anyone in your life facing what you faced? Reflect on how your story might reach them.

________________________________________________________________________

________________________________________________________________________

________________________________________________________________________

________________________________________________________________________

________________________________________________________________________

Sharing your journey deepens your experience of transformation. As you see your story through the reflection of others, you can grow further by engaging in conversations. Others have the opportunity to grow and journey alongside you. You have the ability to encourage others to commence their journey of discovery. Recounting the processes you have gone through allows others to confront their feelings of intimidation or fear about their inner experiences. Your authoritative story is an instructive demonstration of how to build the pathway of a heroic journey.

Sharing your experiences and what is important to you is an effective way to continue your learning and connect with those around you. Providing opportunities for others to share their stories can help those who feel lost when confronted by the unexpected. By sharing your experiences, you can help others find their voice.

*David had lost his brother to suicide ten years ago, and he had never forgiven himself for not being there when his brother needed him the most. The guilt had been weighing heavily on him, and he was still struggling to come to terms with the tragedy. He had tried talking to his friends and family, but he just couldn't shake off the feeling that he could have done more to save his brother.*

*It wasn't until he met Malcolm, a volunteer grief counselor, that he started to see things differently. Malcolm too had lost someone close. With Malcolm's help, David was able to make a new place for his pain and suffering and find a new perspective on the situation. He learned to be kinder to himself and started to see the good in his life again. It wasn't an easy journey, but David was glad to have the example of Malcolm's journey to guide his pathway.*

Although sharing may be uncomfortable at first, its lasting impact is empowering and liberating. You have the freedom to share your story in the way that is best suited for you. Whether it is talking with one friend, a trusted group of friends, or a coworker; writing; or recording a podcast, your journey will bring value to others and create moments of belonging.

Your life journey is not all about the pursuit of success. By pursuing your values and passions, you are finding your authentic self. Sharing your journey allows you to discover who you are in the reflections of others and reaffirms your beliefs and values, boosting your confidence and pushing you on your journey of self-discovery

*Madelyn had always been a private person, keeping her personal life out of public view. She was especially nervous about sharing her divorce with others, fearing judgment and shame. But as time went on, Madelyn realized that her reluctance to open up was holding her back from fully embracing her new life. She needed to forgive herself for the mistakes she had made and the pain she had caused herself and her family.*

*Slowly but surely, Madelyn began to share her story with her closest friends. She was amazed at how supportive and understanding they were, and how they encouraged her to move forward and pursue what truly mattered to her. As she opened up more, Madelyn found that her journey of self-discovery became more enriching and fulfilling. Others who had hidden their monsters began to open up and deal with their work when she shared her story. She started to see the value of pursuing her passions and values and how the pursuit was leading her to become her most authentic self. Through sharing her journey, Madelyn discovered a newfound confidence and sense of purpose.*

Sharing your journey helps you broaden your own sense of purpose by helping others pursue their purpose in the context of whatever challenges or stage of life they are facing. It shines a light for others and serves as a pathway for those in similar predicaments. Sharing how you met your challenges and encouraging others to apply those skills creatively to their problems can help them overcome tough times. Your journey demonstrates courage in how you dealt with discomfort, struggles, and pain. Sharing your journey out of darkness is inspiring and can serve as a roadmap for others. It helps you reflect, broaden your perspective, and understand better the lesson you have been applying. Sharing your journey also keeps you grounded and helps you absorb new lessons. There is always the opportunity to review, challenge, and renew your understanding of your journey.

Sharing your story of self-forgiveness shows others how you have reconciled with what was driving your internal grievances. You have demonstrated the power of a restorative process that can transform lives. Your testimony bears witness to the resilience of your spirit and becomes a light for the pathways of others, creating a community of acceptance, compassion, and hope. Your sharing may encourage others to share with you in a reciprocal way, adding to your store of wisdom. It creates a safe environment for others to share stories with you, connecting you both on a deeper level. You and others will know that you are never alone. You learn that secrets are better when shared, and you teach others to drop burdens they do not have to carry.

You have learned how to trust yourself, explore your dreams, fears, insecurities, or frustrations freely, and to know that being yourself is always enough. It feels terrific to be truly seen and accepted by others. So begin opening up and share your story.

CHAPTER 9

# Live a Life of Self-Forgiveness

You are courageously embarking on a new stage of your self-discovery journey. Self-forgiveness allows you to fundamentally shift how you approach failures and successes. The processes you have practiced are all available to you to apply and refine as you continue to face life and all its challenges. By following this path, you have shown great courage and determination to create a better life for yourself. The skills and techniques you have learned in this workbook enable you to navigate with a newfound sense of purpose and direction.

You have worked to identify and unravel the stories that have held you back. By practicing how to free yourself from the toxic, automatic patterns associated with these stories, you can face whatever surfaces. With acceptance, making room for the discomfort of pain and allowing it to reveal new perspectives on your life experience, you have a tool for life.

Because setbacks are a natural part of your experience, you have learned how your inner critic can turn challenges into toxic inner turmoil. With the lens of self-compassion, you can see these experiences with kindness, care, and understanding. By acknowledging your feelings without judging yourself, allowing the space to feel what you are feeling, and being gentle and kind to yourself, you have a way to respond to toxic self-talk. With respect for your experience, you can open to new perspectives on what was being criticized. Perspective taking examines each element of a toxic story with kindness, care, and understanding. Then both the setbacks and your responses can add to your journey of discovery. You are constantly developing new skills that open you to alternate perspectives that enable you to navigate life with flexibility.

Having perspective is a skill you have practiced engaging in self-forgiveness. Freeing yourself from fixed points of view allows you to step outside your current perspective and view your story from different angles. This freedom gives you insights into new ways forward that are more in touch with your values. Living informed by self-forgiveness is a continuous journey of learning. New challenges and opportunities to grow arise all along the way. You have been uncovering your own truths, and you have come to understand the underlying power of your values.

You are becoming your own wise person. Your inner critic has transformed into your counsel. What you are applying through responding in new and more rewarding ways when you encounter old patterns and challenges is a deep source of learning. Your values are your compass for navigating your life journey and the challenges you face. You have practiced clarifying what matters most to you. Informed by your values, you can now choose options that take you toward meaning and purpose. This is a foundation for an authentic and fulfilling life. Your values point toward the actions you need to take to seek what you truly treasure.

You have used meditative practice, reflective practice, rewriting your story, inner dialogue, and other forms of practice based on your values to engage with and transform your toxic experience. In living your valued life and exercising your talents in the way that only you can, you approach your unique meaning and purpose. Living your authentic life with your unique insight will truly enrich the world around you. Self-forgiveness is a key to unlocking these riches.

The decision to grant yourself forgiveness has undoubtedly had a powerful transformative effect on your life. By continuously applying the skills to forgive yourself, you gain a new appreciation of your life journey and all its lessons. These skills allow you to live more fully in the present moment. Self-forgiveness gives you the ability to create a life with value, based on your unique contribution.

You have faced complexity on this journey, in that your stories each have served some sort of purpose and so you likely resisted letting go of them. Deeply ingrained emotions, responses, and their reinforcing patterns may have been protective in some way. Your inner critic may be very well practiced and highly automatic. However, you devoted time to identify and embrace your monster. You have been vulnerable by being open to your flaws and mistakes. All this has required a values-based response to confront previously toxic experiences. You had the courage to face what was scary and or uncomfortable and work through it to fully engage self-forgiveness.

Granting genuine self-forgiveness is not just a onetime process. Instead, it is an ongoing practice. Each step will continue to bring the challenges and responsibilities of creation and destruction, success and failure. However, you now have skills you can practice to become increasingly proficient and effective in your responses to life's challenges. This practice will allow you to challenge complacency and procrastination. Self-forgiveness will allow you to take appropriate and effective action. Genuine forgiveness will enable you to restore, make restitution, and recover from setbacks as you continue practicing skills that work in the real world.

In living your valued life and exercising your talents in the way that only you can, you will enrich the world around you. You may find others who can benefit from the wisdom you have uncovered in your journey. The gift of your journey of meaning and purpose is a valuable contribution to the world, and it has the power to inspire and enrich others for years to come.

Self-forgiveness is an ongoing journey of renewal, self-discovery, and growth. You now have a set of skills you can use to navigate challenges with renewed purpose and direction. Thank you for taking this journey of discovery through self-forgiveness. All the best on your continued path, full of growth and self-discovery.

The world is a better place with you in it.

# Acknowledgments

My journey of discovery has been traveled with many heroic companions who have been faithful in their support, honest in their reflections, and vulnerable in their own journeys of discovery. Jan, Gharad, and Jordan have loved and supported me in ways beyond telling. Michael, Bernie, Russ, Peter, Paul, Anna, Carly, Erin, Lan Anh, Maggie, Chris, and Heather have given of their treasure of wisdom and insight to inform, guide, and teach me this way. I thank all those who have shared their stories with me.

Finally, Jo-ann has brought to me her deep and ancient knowledge of the journey of healing and renewal, with a love that cannot be surpassed, to bring this message to you. The message, that if heard, embraced, and enacted, is the gateway to your authentic life.

# References

Barnes-Holmes, D., S. C. Hayes, and S. Dymond. 2001. "Self and Self-Directed Rules." In *Relational Frame Theory: A Post-Skinnerian Account of Human Language and Cognition*, edited by Steven C. Hayes, Dermot Barnes-Holmes, and Bryan Roche. Hingham, MA: Kluwer Academic Publishers.

Bennett, R. 2015. "Self-Acceptance: The Compassionate Alternative to Self-Esteem." Presented at ACBS Annual World Conference 13, Berlin, July.

Brown, B. 2010. "The Power of Vulnerability." TEDx: Houston, 20:03. https://www.ted.com/talks/brene_brown_the_power_of_vulnerability.

———. 2015. "Bravery and Authenticity in a Digital World." Chase Jarvis LIVE. https://www.youtube.com/watch?v=cUuXDZERxrk.

Frankl, V. 1985. *Man's Search for Meaning*. New York: Simon and Schuster.

Harris, R. 2006. "Embracing Your Demons: An Overview of Acceptance and Commitment Therapy." *Psychotherapy in Australia* 12(4): 70-6.

———. 2011. *The Happiness Trap: Stop Struggling, Start Living*. Boulder, CO: Shambhala Publications.

———. 2012. *The Reality Slap: Finding Peace and Fulfillment When Life Hurts*. Oakland, CA: New Harbinger Publications.

———. 2019. *ACT Made Simple: An Easy-to-Read Primer on Acceptance and Commitment Therapy*. Oakland, CA: New Harbinger Publications.

Hayes, S. C. 2016. "Psychological Flexibility: How Love Turns Pain into Purpose." TEDx: University of Nevada, 19:39. https://singjupost.com/transcript-how-love-turns-pain-into-purpose-by-steven-hayes.

———. 2019. *A Liberated Mind: The Essential Guide to ACT*. New York: Random House.

Kolts, R. L. 2016. *CFT Made Simple: A Clinician's Guide to Practicing Compassion-Focused Therapy*. Oakland, CA: New Harbinger Publications.

McHugh, L., I. Stewart, and P. Almada. 2019. *A Contextual Behavioral Guide to the Self: Theory and Practice*. Oakland, CA: New Harbinger Publications.

Rogers, C. 1942. *Counseling and Psychotherapy*. Cambridge, MA: Riverside Press.

Villatte, J., and M. Villatte. 2013. "Clinical RFT: Fostering a Flexible Sense of Self." Presented at ACBS World Conference 11, Sydney, July.

Villatte, M., J. Villatte, and S. C. Hayes. 2016. *Mastering the Clinical Conversation: Language as Intervention*. New York: Guilford Press.

Wenzel, M., L. Woodyatt, and K. Hedrick. 2012. "No Genuine Self-Forgiveness Without Accepting Responsibility: Value Reaffirmation as a Key to Maintaining Positive Self-Regard." *European Journal of Social Psychology* 42(5): 617-27.

Woodyatt, L., and M. Wenzel. 2014. "A Needs-Based Perspective on Self-Forgiveness: Addressing Threat to Moral Identity as a Means of Encouraging Interpersonal and Intrapersonal Restoration." *Journal of Experimental Social Psychology* 50(1): 125-35.

**Grant Dewar, PhD**, is a Life Educator, work health and safety adviser, and trainer from Adelaide, South Australia. After losing his father to suicide, Dewar embarked on a life journey to seek better responses and solutions to the devastating effects of self-harm on individuals and the community. Work in the community, public service, and later in life as a health professional has helped him to develop, research, and apply his work on self-forgiveness.

Foreword writer **Russ Harris** is an internationally acclaimed acceptance and commitment therapy (ACT) trainer; and author of the best-selling ACT-based self-help book, *The Happiness Trap*, which has sold more than one million copies and been published in thirty languages.

## Did you know there are **free tools** you can download for this book?

Free tools are things like **worksheets**, **guided meditation exercises**, and **more** that will help you get the most out of your book.

You can download free tools for this book—whether you bought or borrowed it, in any format, from any source—from the New Harbinger website. All you need is a NewHarbinger.com account. Just use the URL provided in this book to view the free tools that are available for it. Then, click on the "download" button for the free tool you want, and follow the prompts that appear to log in to your NewHarbinger.com account and download the material.

You can also save the free tools for this book to your **Free Tools Library** so you can access them again anytime, just by logging in to your account! Just look for this button on the book's free tools page.

**+ Save this to my free tools library**

If you need help accessing or downloading free tools, visit **newharbinger.com/faq** or contact us at **customerservice@newharbinger.com.**